Haunted Places
of
Nottinghamshire

Rupert Matthews

COUNTRYSIDE BOOKS
NEWBURY, BERKSHIRE

COUNTRYSIDE BOOKS
3 Catherine Road
Newbury, Berkshire

To view our complete range of books,
please visit us at
www.countrysidebooks.co.uk

ISBN 1 85306 924 8
EAN 978 1 85306 924 6

Photographs by the author

Designed by Peter Davies, Nautilus Design
Produced through MRM Associates Ltd., Reading
Typeset by Jean Cussons Typesetting, Diss, Norfolk
Printed by Arrowsmith, Bristol

·Contents·

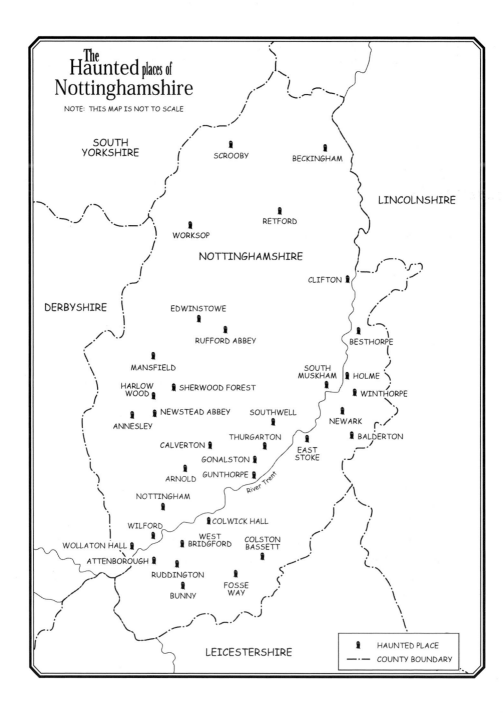

•Introduction•

Nottinghamshire lies at the very heart of England. Not only is it physically near the centre of the country, but it can show almost every facet of our kingdom to stunning effect. There are beautiful rolling hills, sheer cliffs and dark forests of astonishing antiquity. There have been farms here for millennia. There have been factories, mills and mines. And now there are railways, motorways, towns and villages.

And there are ghosts.

These are not strange phenomena that stand out from the fabric of the county, but are part of the place itself. They do not seem out of place for the simple reason that they are not. These are the ghosts of Nottinghamshire people from ages past – and from our own day. They are as much a part of the county as is Nottingham Castle, Sherwood Forest or the open countryside.

There is the lady dressed in blue who walks through the grounds of Worksop Priory. She has been mistaken for a real person more than once, though her alarming habit of vanishing into thin air soon shows she is a ghost. And the ghostly girl who plays happily in Retford seems blissfully unaware of her earthly demise. In Beckingham a black dog forever patrols its chosen route from church to river.

Of course, there are people who say that ghosts don't exist. But if they take the trouble to tour the haunted places of Nottinghamshire and talk to the people who have seen the ghosts and spectres that frequent this haunted county, they might change their minds. They might even see a ghost themselves, for the phantoms of Nottinghamshire are among the most active in the kingdom.

So take your courage in your hands and set out to explore this lovely English county. You never know what you might find – or what might find you!

Rupert Matthews

A ghost dating from coaching days lurks in the old courtyard of the White Hart in Retford (see page 16).

BECKINGHAM

The Black Dog of Beckingham is a ferocious and terrifying beast.

The little village of Beckingham is now bypassed by the busy A631 dual carriageway, allowing the ancient heart of the village to retain its quiet, rural charm. Time was, however, when the main road west from Gainsborough to Sheffield ran through the centre of the village. For one phantom resident at least, the old road retains its attractions.

Running down the Old Trent Road from the village church to the damp water meadows is sometimes seen a colossal black dog. This beast stands as tall as a man's shoulder and has eyes that seem to burn with a strange, inner fire of a dull red colour – as if they were lit by glowing coals. This disturbing phantom has been seen emerging from the churchyard, padding purposefully along the road and turning off near the Old Boatyard to cross the water meadows beside the River Trent, heading south.

Some say that this black dog is the ghost of a monstrously powerful guard dog that belonged to the lord of the manor way back in the days when Christianity was first coming to Nottinghamshire in the early 7th century. Despite its owner's pagan religion, the dog deserted him to follow the missionary priest who came here to convert the locals. When the dog died, the priest buried it in the churchyard as his first convert. Ever since, the dog has returned in spectral form to guard the churchyard against the Devil, evil spirits and pagan deities.

Whatever the origins of the ghostly hound of Beckingham, it is probably better not to confront it. It does not respond kindly to mortals who seek to block its path or impede its determined journey from church to river. Many years ago a man from Gainsborough is said to have tried to stop the ghostly dog by standing in its path and demanding to know its business. The dog glared angrily at the man, who fell down in a faint and was found some hours later lying senseless in the road. He was paralysed down one side of his body and never fully recovered.

Clearly this is an apparition it is best to avoid. So it is as well that the dog follows the old road where there is scarcely any traffic to bother it, rather than the new road.

SCROOBY

Like Beckingham, Scrooby once stood on the main road but is now bypassed. In fact it has been bypassed twice. This haphazard jumble of old houses, pub and church once stood astride the Great North Road that links London to Edinburgh.

When motorised traffic became common, a new road was built around the village to avoid a narrow, tight corner between two houses. Then, in the later 20th century, what was by then called the A1 was bypassed again when the

Just outside Scrooby, the old Great North Road was the site of a murder and a hanging – but which led to the haunting?

multi-lane highway the A1(M) was built to carry the thundering mass of traffic streaming north and south endlessly day and night.

The ghost of Scrooby, however, dates from the days when motorised traffic was undreamed of, and when the first attempt to improve the Great North Road was being made. In theory the upkeep of roads was the business of the parish councils, but the parish council of Scrooby, along with other parishes that lay on main roads, rightly objected that most of the wear and tear was caused by travellers that had nothing to do with the local area. They sometimes received payments from the king's government to repair the road, but not often enough.

To try to solve the problems, Parliament allowed private individuals or companies to take over the maintenance of main roads. They were allowed to charge tolls on users to raise the money to pay for the road repairs, and generate a tidy profit for themselves. Because the gates that barred the road to stop travellers until they paid very often resembled pikes, the arrangement was commonly called a turnpike.

One such turnpike stood just outside Scrooby. Travellers on the Great North Road had to stop to pay for the privilege of using the road. The cash was stored in the tollkeeper's cottage inside a strong box, and from time to time the company banker came by to take the money.

One fateful night in 1779 a local ne'er-do-well by the name of John Spencer decided that he needed the money more than did the turnpike company. He waited until all was dark and still, before letting himself in to the tollkeeper's cottage and lifting the strong box on to his shoulders. He was not as quiet as he should have been, and the tollkeeper woke up. In the fight that followed both the tollkeeper and his wife were killed, but John Spencer failed to make a quick enough getaway. Villagers alerted by the sounds of the fight came running and managed to overpower him in the road.

Spencer could expect little mercy in that day and age. His trial at Retford was brief, then he was dragged back to the scene of his crime and hanged beside the Great North Road at Scrooby. His body was left to hang in chains for weeks, to remind passers-by of the stern justice handed down by the magistrates of Nottinghamshire.

The scene of the execution has long been haunted. The figure of a man in a long, dark coat is seen loitering beside the road. Some motorists have mistaken him for a hitchhiker and pulled up, only to find the mysterious man has vanished. It is not entirely clear if the ghost is of Spencer or of his victim. But whoever's ghost this is, he seems most persistent and may appear in any weather at any time of the day or night.

WORKSOP

The town of Worksop is an ancient one and its museum has finds dating back to the distant Bronze Age. The site has been home to a thriving centre of population ever since – even the dark days of the collapse of the Roman Empire and the Viking onslaught could not ruin Worksop.

It is appropriate, therefore, that Worksop should lay claim to one of the oldest ghosts of Nottinghamshire. In 1103 the Black Canons came here to establish a priory on the southern fringes of the town. They dedicated their house to St Cuthbert and built a solid church in the Norman style with two great towers flanking the west façade. The church has been altered many times since, most recently in 1973, but the twin towers still rear up to dominate the surrounding land.

The priory church's ghost may be a Black Canon from the Middle Ages when this was one of the wealthiest religious houses in the county.

The tower of the priory church at Worksop is haunted by a very athletic ghost.

It is on top of one of these towers that the ghost is seen. He appears only late at night, usually after midnight, and is clearly in a state of high excitement – or possibly fear. He is seen to run around the top of the tower, peering over the wall as if watching something quite disturbing. Some say he jumps up and down as well as running back and forth. That this is a ghostly monk, none who have seen it doubt for a moment. But why he behaves as he does is quite unknown.

The Blue Lady of Worksop is reported to wear robes of 15th century date.

Equally unknown is the reality behind the stories of an underground tunnel that is said to run from the priory gatehouse to the site of the castle, some 2 miles away. Tales from the 19th century talk about a schoolboy who went down the tunnel and never returned except in spectral form, but there is no sign of a tunnel to be seen today. Since nobody has ever excavated the area, the story remains just a legend.

As if that were not enough mystery and supernatural activity, there is yet another ghost that is seen with some frequency in the grounds of the priory. This is of a lady in a blue dress. She is glimpsed most often walking from the gatehouse to the church, and is said to walk with a sprightly spring in her step as she passes along the avenue of mature trees.

This Blue Lady was seen most recently in the autumn of 2004 by a chef walking home late one night from his work at one of the restaurants in the town. When she first appeared, he took little notice as he thought her to be some fellow late-night worker on her way home. But then she vanished into thin air right in front of his eyes. At the time of writing, the man has still not summoned up the courage to take the short cut through the priory grounds again after dark.

The style of this ghost's dress might date her to the later medieval period, though why a woman should trot lightly through the grounds of a monastery is obscure.

The cause of the haunting along the banks of the canal just north of the priory is rather clearer, the ghost itself more substantial. The spectre appears as a young lady, wearing a long dress of a pale colour and with a thick woollen shawl drawn over her head and tied, or clasped, beneath her chin. Her head is bowed and her face can never be clearly seen. She walks in total silence along the banks of the canal and then, as she approaches the bridge in Priorswell Road, she fades swiftly from view. This is the ghost of a young woman whose body was pulled from the canal in the 1870s. Whether she had committed suicide or died as a result of an accident was unclear, though there were no marks of violence on the body. The name of the girl was kept out of the papers, but it has long been rumoured that she was the daughter of a prosperous local family.

Whatever the sad truth behind her death, it seems the girl's ghost cannot rest and returns night after night to retrace her last, fatal walk down to the dark waters of the canal.

*   *   *

The rear entrance to Worksop's Lion Hotel, perhaps the most actively haunted place in the town.

There can be no doubt about the cause of the haunting at the Lion Hotel, now refurbished and part of the Best Western chain. The ghost here is Alice, a girl employed as a servant back in the early 18th century. She had the misfortune to fall desperately in love with the then owner of the hotel. As a prosperous businessman, he had his eyes on a richer dowry and refused to have anything to do with an impoverished, if pretty, servant. Distraught, the girl hanged herself.

The phantom girl is encountered in the older part of the hotel, most often in the corridor over the archway that connects the yard to the street, or on the staircase leading down from the corridor to the bar. She also frequents the kitchen, though she is not seen there so often. When she does put in an appearance, she can be a real nuisance. She bangs doors, throws open the fridge door and moves utensils around when nobody is looking.

More sinister is her behaviour upstairs in room 201, a bedroom not often rented out to the public and usually used by off-duty staff. One lady staff worker was resting in the room in the summer of 2002 when she woke up with a start. The atmosphere was hot and oppressive, and she could not breathe. The sense of suffocation was as if a pair of hands were pushing down hard on the chest, stopping any breath being taken. After a few seconds, the feeling passed and the temperature of the room returned to normal. A most disturbing experience.

*　　*　　*

The National Trust maintains an odd little property in the form of 'Mr Straw's House', otherwise known as No 7 Blyth Grove. Although, at first sight, identical to thousands of other Edwardian town houses to be found in Worksop and across the country, what makes this place unique is that after the death of Mr William Straw in the early 1930s, his son and heir, Walter, refused absolutely to have any changes made to the house. He lived the life of a recluse until his death, when the property was acquired by the National Trust.

The Trust keeps the house in its pristine original condition, only undertaking necessary repairs. It has period wallpaper, furniture and garden, while the only heating is by way of open fires and lighting is by gas.

The identity of the ghost is not hard to guess. It must be Mr Straw, either senior or junior. He walks noisily around his old home, presumably to ensure that still nothing has been changed. He is heard more often than seen, his footsteps changing clearly in tone as they move from carpet to floorboards and back again.

*   *   *

Five miles south-east of Worksop stands another National Trust property with a ghost: Clumber Park. The magnificent, sweeping grounds of almost 4,000 acres are open daily, showing off over 120 types of tree, a Victorian Gothic chapel and, of course, the ghost.

Seen most often near the magnificent serpentine lake, lingering on the balustraded bridge or flitting around the delightful Doric temple, this phantom is said to be a lady dressed in a long coat or cloak of grey or pale brown. She does not stay in sight for long and fades rapidly from view if anyone gets too close.

RETFORD

The attractive town of Retford was for centuries the main market centre for northern Nottinghamshire. Although Worksop is now larger in terms of population, Retford has managed to retain its atmosphere as a bustling, busy place for shopping. In terms of the supernatural, however, the two towns are well matched.

The first ghost to be met at Retford is to be found at the Little Theatre, located just off the ring road that carries through traffic around the historic heart of the town. It stands in Wharf Road and backs onto the Chesterfield Canal. Although the building dates from the 1970s, it stands on the site of a warehouse and dock that serviced the boats bringing goods to the town by water in days gone by. The ghost would seem to belong to this earlier building rather than to the theatre.

The old building has long been rumoured to be haunted, though by whom or by what it is not now easy to discover. The modern theatre, however, is sometimes host to the apparition of a man dressed in black. Some who see him think he is wearing a dinner suit, others that it is a normal day suit, though made in black cloth. And there are other odd happenings. A part of the auditorium will suddenly become freezingly cold for no apparent reason and disembodied footsteps have been heard. Whoever the ghost may be, he does not seem to cause much trouble and certainly does nothing to stop the audience enjoying the excellent quality of shows put on here.

*   *   *

The historic heart of Retford is The Square. It is here that markets were held at which livestock and farm produce were sold. The impressive 13th century church of St Swithun stands at its north-east corner, while the north-west corner is the site of the White Hart. This welcoming pub was once a coaching inn, providing food, drink and warmth to the passengers on the regular stagecoaches running up the Great North Road, which then passed through the town.

It was one of these large, heavy coaches that inadvertently caused the first of the hauntings to be found in the White Hart. While the passengers were inside slaking their thirsts, the driver and the hotel grooms were trying to get fresh horses hitched to the coach to take it swiftly on the next stage of its journey. Tragically, one of the horses was restive and, when put into the traces, reared and plunged with great violence. The horse suddenly pushed the coach backward, crushing a little girl against the wall of the inn. She died of her injuries later that day.

The ghostly girl seems quite happy in the courtyard. She trots and runs about as if enjoying some marvellous game that gives her great enjoyment. More than one person has mistaken her for a real girl in fancy dress and has been startled when she suddenly vanishes into thin air.

As a memorial to the poor child, a bust of her was made and erected high above the bar in the main front room of the White Hart. It is still there, and with good reason for the little statue had a curse laid upon it by the girl's father. If ever the bust were removed from the hotel, he said, death would swiftly follow. Even touching the statue would bring bad luck. It must remain, the man decreed, as a dire warning to coach drivers and ostlers to be more careful in future.

In 1998 the White Hart was undergoing refurbishment and redecoration. The landlady gave the workmen strict instructions to leave the cursed statue well alone, but to work around it with whatever modern electrics or styling was deemed necessary. Despite such clear instructions, however, one workman proved to be dangerously careless. He knocked the statue with the end of his ladder and chipped it. Almost instantaneously the ceiling of the bar collapsed with a terrific crash. This was all the more strange as the surveyor had guaranteed only a few days earlier that the ceiling was structurally sound and would need nothing more than a lick of paint in the refurbishment. The ceiling was replaced, but this time the workmen erected a box around the statue to ensure that no more accidents took place.

The cursed statue of the White Hart is now kept safely locked in a display case, for bad luck comes if she is disturbed.

But the White Hart has one more phantom. High up at the very apex of the roof is a small chamber with a window that looks down on the courtyard. Sometimes the face of a young woman is seen peering from the room at the merry drinkers and diners enjoying the hospitality of the pub below. And light footsteps may be heard along the narrow, low corridor that leads to the room. This female phantom is said to be the guardian spirit of the inn, who keeps the pub safe and prosperous. The door to the chamber is now nailed shut. The

The topmost window of the White Hart harbours a strange spirit, and the room behind is now permanently locked.

barman on duty in the winter months of 2004 considered that it was best to leave the ghost in peace.

*　　*　　*

Across The Square from the White Hart is the Town Hall. The downstairs of the building is dominated by a great, sweeping staircase, which leads up to the Council Chamber and various offices. This staircase, and one of the private offices upstairs, is haunted by a Victorian lawyer. He appears in wig and gown as if on his way to some important court appearance, but seems in no great hurry as he strolls nonchalantly through the room and down the stairs. After all, whatever case he was involved with must have ended many decades ago.

*　　*　　*

West of the River Idle on what was once the Great North Road, but is now merely the A638, stands the imposing and comfortable West Retford Hotel. This occupies what was until the early 20th century West Retford House, a beautiful 18th century mansion. The hotel has a fine restaurant and comfortable rooms to attract customers, and prides itself on seasonal and festive events.

The ghost here is very active, but does not seem to cause anybody any real bother or trouble. The haunting has gone on as long as the building has been a hotel and, so staff say, was the cause of the house being converted to an hotel in the first place.

Back around the time of the Great War, the man who owned the house was often away on war work. While he was absent the lady of the house found a cure for her boredom and relief from her loneliness in some exceptionally un-ladylike activity with a burly, good-looking

Retford Town Hall is haunted by a lawyer from Victorian days.

The staircase where the phantom is seen most often.

stablehand. Of course, gossip quickly ran through the town about the illicit affair. News reached the husband, who stormed back to Retford in a foul temper. Within two days the stablehand had committed suicide – or at least so the coroner decided – by hanging himself in the stables, and the wayward wife had been packed off to stay with her mother in some remote village. For a few years the betrayed owner of the house kept the property, though he did not stay there often. Then the run-down building was put

The commanding frontage of the West Retford Hotel, where the ghost recalls a tragedy from the time when this was a private house.

up for sale. It was bought by a businessman for conversion to a hotel. Strangely, although the contents had been auctioned off before the house was sold, a portrait of a lady in a white dress was found thrown carelessly aside in an upstairs bedroom. It is thought to be a portrait of the unfaithful wife and now hangs over the staircase.

But the portrait is not the only reminder of the adulterous affair of almost a century ago. The ghost is still here. There can be no doubt that this is the ghost of the errant wife, for she is seen often in what is now a function room called the Rufford Room, but was in the past the master bedroom of the house. She sometimes leaves the chamber, walks down the fine staircase over which hangs the mysterious portrait, turns right to pass through the reception hall and goes through the exit leading down to a side door that gives access to the old stables.

The phantom then glides swiftly across the courtyard to vanish just outside the stables, now converted into luxurious suites for guests.

Of course, the ghost is not always seen tracing her complete ghostly journey, but only part of it. She is noticed most frequently passing through reception, for a member of staff is on duty there day and night. The door has been seen to fly open, then slam shut more than once. Mysteriously on one occasion it performed this trick when the night porter had locked it securely only half an hour earlier. Presumably the ghost was not to be frustrated by something as mundane as a mortal lock and key.

The mysterious portrait at the West Retford Hotel. Is this the ghost?

She is also seen very often on the staircase. In the spring of 2004 a chambermaid came around the corner to go upstairs to clean the bedrooms when she saw a lady coming down. Not realising it was the ghost, she stepped aside to allow the guest, as she thought, to pass by. But the figure had vanished completely. Only then did she realise that she had seen the phantom lady in white.

CLIFTON

The villages of North and South Clifton stand on a low ridge just east of the River Trent, and it is the river that gives this place its supernatural link.

The large Clifton Hall, still a private house, was for some 600 years home to the Clifton family, who owned both villages and vast spreading estates in this

The ornamental gates of Clifton church, which stands above the water meadow that was formerly the venue for a supernatural beast.

area of Nottinghamshire. Although the family enjoyed their lands for so many years, they were not without their troubles. The River Trent was periodically home to a monstrous fish, which swam upstream to reach the water meadow spreading out just below the church that serves both villages.

There the strange beast would splash around, threaten villagers and generally make a nuisance of itself. The purpose of the fish, variously described as being carp or sturgeon shaped but as large as a dolphin, was to announce the death of the current head of the Clifton family. After the death took place, the new arrival would turn tail and head downstream.

Another legend connected to the Trent, which was formerly believed widely in Nottinghamshire and beyond, was that the river demanded three human lives each year. No matter how careful boatmen or travellers might be, three of them would die in the swirling waters of one of England's longest rivers. Some have speculated that this belief dates back to pagan times when the powerful river god may have actually received human sacrifices. It is impossible to be certain, but the druids certainly held the Trent in high respect.

•Central Nottinghamshire•

EDWINSTOWE

The gigantic Major Oak is the focus for hauntings in the woods around Edwinstowe.

The little town of Edwinstowe lies in the heart of ancient Sherwood Forest, so it is apt that stories of Robin Hood abound here.

The charming 12th century church, for instance, is said to be the place where Robin married Maid Marion one summer's day after he was pardoned for his outlaw ways by King Richard the Lionheart. Two miles north-west of the town is a huge hollow oak tree, known locally as Robin Hood's Larder. It is said that the outlaw used to hang his poached deer from the upper branches so that they would mature nicely before being eaten.

A second oak, the largest in England, stands north of the town and goes by the name of the Major Oak. This tree, too, is linked to Robin Hood as it is said to have been the spot where he had his main camp in the forest. It is here that the Sherwood Forest Visitor Centre has been built with its car park, cafeteria and displays. Although the forest once spread from Nottingham to Mansfield, this area contains probably the oldest trees and may be as close to the woodland known to Robin Hood as the modern world can get.

Robin Hood apart, the woods around the Major Oak are haunted by a strange entity. It does not seem to have any definite form, but it is most definitely unfriendly. Some people walking the paths around here have felt that something is following them and have the distinct impression that they are unwelcome. They leave hurriedly.

RUFFORD ABBEY

The tumbling ruins of Rufford have been roofless for less than a century. It was founded as a Cistercian monastery in the 12th century, becoming a private home after the dissolution of the monasteries by King Henry VIII in the 1540s.

Over the centuries the Abbey was changed, altered and rebuilt numerous times so that very little of the original structure remains. Then, in the 1930s, it fell into disrepair and neglect. Today only part of the once luxurious home remains intact, housing a craft centre, restaurant and various exhibits. The rest is empty and roofless, though the surrounding 500 acre park is much used by local families, dog walkers and joggers. And with reason, for this is one of the finest parks in Nottinghamshire.

The ruins of Rufford Abbey.

The Abbey is now run by Nottinghamshire County Council and makes quite a feature of its hauntings. Ghost Hunter Dinners are held which provide a hearty meal followed by a hunt for the site's spectres with investigative equipment.

Perhaps the most active ghost is the Black Friar. This phantom is truly terrifying. He will walk up to witnesses, his cowl pulled down to hide his face, but on getting close will lift his head to flick back the cowl to reveal a grinning skull. On 3rd December 1901 an Edwinstowe man visiting Rufford saw the ghostly monk and collapsed in fright; he died soon after.

Rather less startling is the White Lady who flits around the gardens. This is said to be the shade of Lady Arabella Stuart, who spent a happy childhood here before a tragic adult life overtook her. She was born in 1575 the daughter of Elizabeth Cavendish and Charles Lennox, which meant she was distantly in line to the thrones of both England and Scotland. This made her a potential

The gardens of Rufford Abbey are as famous for their roses as for their ghosts.

centre for intrigue, so after her parents' death the teenager was taken in hand by Queen Elizabeth and sent to stay with her grandmother, the Countess of Shrewsbury, who could be relied upon to keep the girl out of the hands of unscrupulous noblemen.

After Elizabeth died, the new King of England, James VI of Scotland, brought Lady Arabella to his court in London where he could keep a close eye on her. He did not watch closely enough, for Arabella fell in love with William Seymour, son of the Earl of Hertford, and married him in secret. The match was politically unwise as it might have been construed as dynastic ambition by the

Seymours. This was certainly how King James saw it, so he separated the couple and sent Lady Arabella to imprisonment in luxury apartments in the Tower of London. She made a bold escape attempt, dressed as a boy, in 1610 but her ship was captured off Dover and she was returned to the Tower. At the age of 40, Lady Arabella died, but her ghost soon returned to Rufford. She has been seen from time to time ever since.

Less dramatic, but equally persistent, is the ghostly nanny dressed in demure Victorian clothes who pushes a pram around the grounds. She is seen often in the summer, but ignores those mortals who approach her and goes on her way.

Rufford must be one of the most haunted sites in Nottinghamshire, if not England. It is certainly one of the most interesting and enjoyable to visit.

MANSFIELD

The industrial town of Mansfield grew rapidly after coal was discovered there, but has been a prosperous enough settlement since well before the Romans came to Britain. The caves in the sandstone cliffs of Southwell Road have yielded prehistoric finds and were inhabited well into the 19th century.

The most active ghost of the town is seen amid the housing estates that sprang up south-east of the old town during the 1930s, though he clearly dates to a much earlier period. Known these days as Timothy, his real name having long been forgotten, he lurks around the traffic lights on the A617 outside the Oak public house, and some claim to have seen him inside the pub itself.

He wears a long coat of a dark, rough material with a generously cut shape and a high collar. Those who see this ghost say he appears upset and moves about as if in a temper or greatly agitated. On a few, rare occasions he will approach a witness to announce 'I did not do it' before fading to nothingness. This behaviour has led some to speculate that the ghost is that of a man hanged on the gibbet that once stood beside the road junction at this spot. If so, it would seem that he was wrongfully convicted and that his distraught phantom returns to announce this fact to an uncaring world.

The road junction in Mansfield that was formerly the site of the town gallows.

Mansfield Woodhouse was once a separate village, but the spreading suburbs of Mansfield have merged the two places. Off one of these estates runs a narrow track that leads into woodland where lie the ruins of Hall Place, a fine Victorian mansion that burned down in the 1950s. Around these atmospheric ruins lurks a ghostly lady in a flowing white gown. She does not restrict her activities to the ruins, but has also been seen downhill near the A60 and even in the grounds of the local secondary school. Who she is and what her story might be are now quite unknown.

The old Palace Theatre in Mansfield long had a reputation for being haunted, but the phantom in the yellow boots seems to have abandoned the site – at the time of writing anyway.

HARLOW WOOD

Some distance south of Mansfield, the A60 to Nottingham runs through an area of dense woodland known as Harlow Wood. This is one of the few stretches of the old Sherwood Forest that has not yet been developed. Tucked away within the trees is a college and a school, yet it is not these modern buildings that are haunted but the road itself. And a real tragedy gave rise to the hauntings.

On 7th July 1817 the 17-year-old Bessie Sheppard left her home in Papplewick to walk to Mansfield to look for work in service. The girl already had some experience of domestic employment and was keen to find a good position. She put on her best dress, a new pair of smart shoes and carried a new umbrella of a bright and distinctive design. Young Bessie found herself work and, at 6 pm, set off to walk home. She never got there.

Next morning her family and neighbours set out to search for Bessie only to find her battered and bloody body thrown in a ditch beside the main road in Harlow Wood. A stout wooden staff, drenched in blood, was found nearby. At once the hunt was on for the killer.

The landlord of the nearby Three Crowns reported that a man had come into the pub on the evening of the murder trying to sell a pair of lady's shoes but had left after failing to find a buyer. He gave a description of the man and, two days later, the same man was seen in Bunny selling a colourful umbrella. The man was arrested next day in Loughborough. He turned out to be a scissor grinder from Sheffield named Charles Rotherham, who had been sacked from his job for laziness. He had failed to find new employment and left Sheffield, apparently to look for work. Rotherham had got only as far as Newstead before drinking away the last of his money. He walked out of the pub in a temper at just the time that the unfortunate Bessie was leaving Mansfield.

There could be no doubt as to Rotherham's guilt. After being sentenced to death, Rotherham told his gaolers that he had attacked the well-dressed Bessie in the hope of getting money, but that once he began hitting her he had been overcome by a frenzied and uncontrollable rage. The good folk of

The sad inscription recalling a murder that gave rise to the haunting of Harlow Wood.

Nottinghamshire believed in swift justice in 1817, so Rotherham was hanged just two weeks after his crime.

Back in Papplewick, Bessie's death had been a shock to the community. She had been a bright, popular girl. Soon a collection was made, with her would-be employers in Mansfield making a generous donation. A stone was erected on the site of the murder and engraved with details of poor Bessie's fate.

The stone stood undisturbed for many years beside the main road through the woods, reminding passers-by of the evils of which men are capable. Gradually the inscription weathered away. But in the 1960s the demands of the increasing speed and numbers of motorcars using the A60 forced the county engineers to widen the road. This took the roadway over the site of the Sheppard Stone, so it was decided to move the stone away from the new road and to replace the worn engraving with an identical message – though for some reason the new inscription used Bessie's real name 'Elizabeth'.

Poor Bessie, however, does not seem to have appreciated the change. Ever since the stone was moved to its new site, motorists have been reporting a strange figure lurking near the spot. The young woman carrying an umbrella seems to be agitated and distressed in some way. Some have thought she is a hitchhiker, others that she is lost but when the drivers stop to offer help, the figure glides off into the woodland and vanishes.

ANNESLEY

Annesley is one of the abandoned villages of Nottinghamshire. It can boast a ruined castle, though little more than the earthworks remain above ground, and a crumbling, roofless church. To the north spread the modern housing estates named Annesley Woodhouse and Annesley Nuncargate, but it is around the old site that the ghosts congregate.

Annesley Hall still stands, set back from the A608 behind the ruined church, and is now a private house. For many years this was the home of the Chaworth family who were distantly related to the Byrons of nearby Newstead Abbey. The two families did not get on and in 1790 the 5th Lord Byron killed William Chaworth in a duel. This was but one of the many crimes that earned the 5th Lord Byron the local nickname of 'Wicked Jack'. No doubt the Chaworths were as relieved as everyone else around Annesley when Wicked Jack dropped dead and the title and estates passed to his 10-year-old great-nephew who had been living in Edinburgh.

The Chaworths, however, were less than impressed when the lame and impoverished new baron fell in love with their daughter Mary. Despite the fact that Byron wrote a startlingly impressive poem *The Bright Morning Star of Annesley* in honour of young Mary, the Chaworths threw him out. Mary went on to make a happy if unpoetic marriage, while Byron matured to be wayward but also one of the finest poets in English history.

Back at Annesley, the Chaworths were soon proving that they were not as noble and superior as they liked to maintain. The then squire got one of his servant girls pregnant. Wanting to avoid a scandal, Squire Chaworth packed the girl off to stay with an aunt in Northumberland. Unlike Wicked Jack Byron, however, Squire Chaworth was no scoundrel. He sent the girl off with a good purse of silver and made sure that regular payments were sent to her as the birth approached. The servant girl could not write, but her aunt could and sent Squire Chaworth regular bulletins.

In due course a healthy boy was born to the girl in Northumberland. Squire Chaworth sent larger sums now to maintain the mother and child. Regular letters came telling him how his illegitimate boy was crawling, had got his first teeth, could say a few words and so forth. Squire Chaworth was delighted when he got a small lock of his boy's hair.

Then one evening a year or so after the birth, the servant girl was seen by a groom in the grounds of Annesley Hall. Appearing to be thin and ill, she was making for the house and ignored the groom when he called out. The man reported what he had seen, but strangely the girl had not arrived at the house. She was seen several times over the following weeks and it became obvious that the girl was a ghost, not a mortal. Eventually the story reached Squire Chaworth. He was still receiving letters from Northumberland with assurances that all was well. At first he did not believe the stories, but then he decided to take action.

He sent his steward up to Northumberland to inquire after the girl and her baby boy. The steward found that the girl had died around the time that her ghost had first appeared. Her aunt had promptly sent the little boy to the workhouse and was pocketing Squire Chaworth's money to fund a boozy lifestyle for herself and her husband. The boy was rescued from the workhouse and sent to live with more honest relatives. Clearly the ghost had come to demand help for her son.

Back at Annesley Hall, however, the ghost was still active. She is seen to this day, wandering the grounds of the Hall and nearby areas. She is said to walk quietly and modestly, wearing a hooded bonnet and shawl.

Another female ghost, or perhaps it is the same spectre, is seen less often. This ghost has long dark hair that she brushes repeatedly as she sits beside a well in the Hall grounds. Lacking a bonnet and shawl she may be a quite different young woman, but if so nobody knows who she is.

Equally obscure is the ghost that lurks around the ruined church. The crumbling structure stands on a small hill beside the main road through the vanished village, though it is all but hidden in a dense clump of trees. A man wearing a black cloak or robe has been seen here. He is usually noticed by passing motorists who report that he crosses the road, then climbs up the hillock towards the church. He is usually referred to as the Black Monk of Annesley, but there was no monastery here.

The ruined church at Annesley is home to a mysterious phantom in black.

Some think he may be a ghostly vicar wearing a cassock. Another theory holds that this is the ghost of James Annesley, who died in the 1760s. He is known to have spent his last years rarely straying from the vicinity of house and church. After his adventures, he probably did not want to leave home again.

His story begins in 1710 when he was a boy of nine. Young James Annesley was at school in Ireland when he suffered a fall, cracked his head open on a stone and fell into a coma. Word was rushed to his father, Baron Arthur Annesley, in England. The baron was held up by business, so he sent his brother Richard to Ireland. Arriving in Ireland, Richard had not even time to reach the school before the boy died. He arranged a funeral, then returned home.

In 1727 Baron Arthur died and Richard inherited the title and estates. Two years later a mysterious disease carried off his cousin the Earl of Anglesey and his son, leaving Richard Annesley as the sole heir to the vast fortune of the Angleseys. He enjoyed his money to the full in a riot of wild, loose living.

Then, in 1742, a man appeared in London saying that he was James Annesley, long thought dead. He claimed the family titles and estates for himself and launched a lawsuit that proved to be both long and tortuous. He said that he had recovered from his coma in Ireland in 1710. The schoolmaster, he explained, had been bribed by Richard to kill him, but had not wanted to murder the boy. Instead, he had sold him into slavery in the American colonies. James's story was that he had grown up on the frontier, fled his plantation slavery and married a girl from the Iroquois tribe. After she died, James had worked as a fur trapper before taking ship as a seaman and engaging in the coastal trade between the West Indies and the New England colonies. He said that, arriving in England as part of a merchant cruise, he had decided to see if he could trace his family. All he could recall with any certainty was the name of his father and the name of his school in Ireland. This, he claimed, should prove enough to identify him.

The court case involved witnesses from the school, from America and from the Annesley estates. In the end, the English courts found that the young man was an imposter, while the Irish courts found that he was genuinely James Annesley. The younger man then came to an arrangement with his disputed wicked uncle. Baron Richard Annesley kept the family titles and estates intact, but James was given private apartments at Annesley and all his living expenses as a gentlemen were paid out of the family coffers. It was generally supposed that he was an illegitimate son of the fourth baron, Arthur.

Whoever he was, he seems devoted to the old ruin, now a listed monument.

NEWSTEAD ABBEY

Newstead Abbey is home to perhaps the most elusive and certainly the most famous ghost of Nottinghamshire – some would say in all England. If the stories are to believed this is an especially powerful, persistent and malevolent haunting. One that it is well to avoid if you possibly can.

It all began in France in a chilly baronial hall warmed by a roaring fire in 1170. Wine and food had flowed freely among the guests, but England's King Henry II was in a furious temper. For eight years he had been locked into a bitter quarrel with the Archbishop of Canterbury, his former friend Thomas à Becket, over the respective rights of Church and Crown. The dispute was astonishingly complex, but Henry was determined to rule over his own kingdom, while Thomas was equally determined to keep the Church faithful only to Christ. This particular day a messenger had come from England to inform Henry that Thomas had once again broken the King's law to enforce what he saw as the Church's rights. In his temper Henry raged, 'Will no one rid me of this turbulent priest?' Four knights took him at his word, rode to Canterbury and killed the Archbishop.

Predictably the Pope, along with all Europe's bishops, abbots and priests were outraged. More seriously for Henry, so was public opinion in England. The king protested his innocence, saying he had not meant his men to kill Thomas, and he set about placating the angry churchmen. Among various other measures, Henry lavished endowments on the Church and established or rebuilt several churches and monasteries. Newstead Abbey was one of the monasteries founded by King Henry. When the foundation stone was laid, the first abbot solemnly laid a curse on any king or royal official who tried to take what had been given in recompense for the sacrilegious crime.

The years passed and centuries rolled away. Newstead Abbey, like many other monasteries, grew wealthy and fat. Then a new King Henry, the eighth, came to the throne. This king had his own arguments with the Pope in Rome and severed England from the Catholic faith. He made himself Head of the Church in England, and declared himself the new owner of the monasteries. Soon afterwards he closed them all down, taking their wealth for himself.

When news came in 1536 that Newstead Abbey was next on the list to be closed, the abbot gathered together all the moveable wealth of the house – the jewelled reliquaries, crosses and communion silver – and hid it somewhere nearby. Perhaps he hoped to return one day soon, should Henry die and a more Catholic monarch come to the throne. Then he found the foundation stone and added his curse to that laid over three centuries earlier.

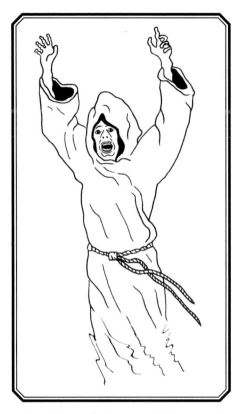

The Goblin-Monk of Newstead Abbey is a truly terrifying phantom.

The abbot conjured up the fearsome phantom Goblin-Monk of Newstead Abbey and charged it to take revenge on any who treated the Abbey with disdain. Then he left, hoping to come back but destined never to return.

The Goblin-Monk remained. He was to be kept busy.

By 1540, workmen hired by King Henry VIII had stripped the church of its lead roof, pillaged the buildings of valuable materials and generally despoiled the place. Then, in 1540, King Henry gave the run-down buildings and the vast estates of the Abbey to one John Byron of nearby Colwick. Mr Byron converted some of the buildings into a country mansion, allowing the rest to fall into ruin. In 1643 a grateful King Charles I raised the family to the peerage in thanks for their help in the Civil War.

All this time the Goblin-Monk put in the occasional appearance. He foretold the death of more than one Baron Byron and a sighting could be relied upon to bring misfortune to whoever saw it. Like all goblins, the Goblin-Monk displayed a malevolence to humanity, quite at odds with the more gentle attitude of the monks. Then, in 1760, he began his work in earnest.

William, the 5th Baron Byron, was out fishing on the lake near the Abbey. He let down a light anchor to keep his boat from drifting and set to work with rod and line. As the day came to an end, he attempted to pull up his anchor, but found it was fouled. After much heaving, tugging and some help from the estate boatman, the Baron hauled up a large brass eagle set on a pillar of brass.

They got the object ashore and called in an antiquary from Nottingham who cleaned it up. The object was revealed as the lectern of the old Abbey, which had been thrown in to the lake by the Abbot at the time of the closure of his house. It was found that the eagle unscrewed from the pillar. Hidden within the watertight compartment were found a mass of parchment documents. These included the original grant from King Henry II to establish the Abbey, various land deeds from the centuries that followed and a few indulgences – documents promising remission from time in Hell that could be sold to credulous believers for ready cash. Lord Byron sold the lectern for equally ready cash. It is now in Southwell Minster, where it is used regularly as a lectern in Christian worship.

The Goblin-Monk was seen several times immediately after the lectern was sold. Presumably he was angry that the old property deeds had been found.

He got even angrier the following summer when a severe drought hit Nottinghamshire. The water level in the lake fell lower than anyone could remember, until far out from the shore, stuck deep in the mud, a great chest was revealed, bound around with iron hoops and straps. Lord Byron at once believed that this was the fabled lost treasure of Newstead Abbey and set about recovering it. Servants were sent out to fetch it, but they sank to their waists in the sticky mud and counted themselves lucky to get out again alive. So as the afternoon wore on horses were brought down to the shore of the lake, hitched up to stout chains and ropes. Boards were laid across the mud, enabling men to walk out to reach the great chest and attach the chains. But no matter how the horses struggled or pulled, the chest would not come free from the mud.

As dusk was falling, Lord Byron sat and thought. He sent messengers to his neighbours asking them to come with their carthorses and plough teams, and promised a share of the treasure for their help.

When the dark, moonless night settled over the landscape, however, the Goblin-Monk walked the lakeshore. The servants posted by Lord Byron to keep watch wisely made themselves scarce. Then it began to rain. And it rained like it had never rained before. Waters flooded down into the lake. First the boards began to float free, then the chest vanished beneath the waves, then the waters rose to overflow their normal banks. Strangely, it did not rain across all of drought-striken Nottinghamshire, only here.

By dawn all hope of recovering the chest had gone.

But the curse of the Goblin-Monk had not. Lord Byron began to suffer a run of ill luck. Business ventures failed. Gambling stakes were lost. He remained childless. As his fortune dwindled he became unable to maintain his ancestral home and soon he was forced to live in the scullery with his one remaining servant as that was the only room that remained watertight. In 1798 he died alone and unmourned.

The estate passed to his great-nephew, George Gordon Byron who was just 10-years-old. Lord George continued to enjoy the bad luck brought on the Byrons by the Goblin-Monk. He led a drunken, dissolute life, which ensured that the family of his great love, Mary Chaworth, refused permission for a marriage. His first efforts at poetry were torn apart by the critics. In 1812 he left Newstead, and at once his luck changed. His writings became popular and sold well. He fell in love again, with Lady Caroline Lamb, and was lionised by London Society.

Then Byron came back to Newstead and again the baleful influence of the Goblin-Monk took hold. Perhaps the phantom was angered when Byron buried his dog, Boatswain, on the site of the abbey's high altar. For whatever reason, the ghost took against the young man once more.

Lady Caroline dropped Byron very publicly – famously saying that he was 'Mad, bad, and dangerous to know'. Things seemed to look up in 1815 when

Newstead Abbey fell into near ruin in the 18th century, but has now been restored to its former glory.

he became engaged to a wealthy heiress named Anne Milbanke. But the night before the wedding the Goblin-Monk walked yet again, this time meeting Lord Byron himself among the ruins of the old abbey. Byron fled, but could not outrun his bad luck. The marriage failed after the birth of a daughter, and Anne returned to her family.

Byron later set down his meeting with the Goblin-Monk, using it in a fictional work as if it appeared to a man named Don Juan, writing:

But lo! A monk, arrayed
In cowl and beads, and dusky garb, appeared
Now in the moonlight, and now lapsed in shade,
With steps that trod as heavy, yet unheard;
His garments only a slight murmur made;
He moved as shadowy as the Sisters Weird,
But slowly; and as he passed Juan by,
Glanced, without pausing, on him a bright eye.

Byron sold the ruined Abbey to Thomas Wildman, an old school friend, for £100,000 and moved abroad. His writings again began to find favour, but before he could cement his fame and fortune he died of marsh fever while fighting alongside the Greeks in their war of independence against the Turkish Empire. His daughter married into the Lovelace family and led a fruitful and happy life.

It was during Colonel Wildman's time that the final phantom came to haunt Newstead Abbey. One day in 1823 a young lady enquired at the Abbey about renting a cottage in the grounds. The lady was well dressed, seemed respectable enough and had cash to pay her rent. She gave her name as Sophia Hyatt, but declined to add any details of her family or home. A person who lived nearby at the time wrote: 'No one knew exactly whence she came nor what were her connexions. Many of her days were passed in rambling about the gardens and grounds of the Abbey, to which, by the kindness of Colonel Wildman, she had free access. Her dress was invariably the same; and she was known by the servants at Newstead as The White Lady. She left an impression in the romantic neighbourhood she resided in; and her singularity will not soon be forgotten.

'One day she copied the inscription from Lord Byron's tablet; took off her bonnet and wiped a string of it on the floor of the vault; then cut a piece away carefully, wrapped it in paper and put it in her pocket; the last rhymes she wrote strangely foreboded, in their closing verse, the melancholy fate which was shortly to befall her:

But 'tis past, and now for ever
Fancy's vision's bliss is o'er;
But to forget thee, Newstead – never,
Though I shall haunt thy shades no more

'Through her deafness she was run over by a cart at the entrance to the Maypole Inn yard, Nottingham, on 28th September, 1825, and unfortunately killed. Colonel Wildman took upon himself the care of her interment, in the churchyard of Hucknall, as near as possible to the vault which contains the body of Lord Byron.'

Lord Byron found fame as a poet, and experienced two ghostly happenings at his family home of Newstead Abbey.

There was gossip that she might have been an illegitimate child of the 5th Baron, or that she was some infatuated admirer of the poet Byron, but nobody really knew. The tale continues: 'The most singular aspect of the unknown lady's stay at Newstead is that, after her interment, she was seen again in the grounds of Newstead; she appeared in her customary clothing and walked with her usual sedate stride. The servants soon knew that The White Lady was back and the tale spread through the neighbourhood; though Colonel Wildman refused to have talk of the figure conducted in his presence.'

The ghost does not seem to have persisted for very long. She is not seen these days.

Another shade that seems to have vanished is the benevolent and friendly monk who once sang plainchant in those areas of the house that had originally been part of the medieval abbey. Byron himself wrote:

But in the noontide of the moon, and when
The winde is winged from one point of heaven
There moans a strange unearthly sound, which then
Is musical – a dying accent driven
Through the huge arch, which soars and sinks again
Some deem it but the distant echo given
Back to the nigh wind by the waterfall
And harmonized by the old choral wall.

Others, that some original shape or form,
Shaped by decay perchance, hath given the power
(Though less than that of Memnon's statue, warm
In Egypt's rays, to harp at a fix'd hour)
To this grey ruin with a voice to charm.
Sad but serene, it sweeps o'er tree or tower:
The cause, I know not, nor can solve; but such
The fact: I've heard it – once perhaps too much.

In 1828 the author Sir Richard Phillips visited Newstead and remembered, 'I walked through and around the building with the poem in my hand.' He stayed the night in the chamber where Lord Byron had heard the phantom music and recorded: 'This apartment is remote from the dormitories of the family, and the ascent to it is by a newel stone staircase. A stranger to personal fear and superstition, I enjoyed my berth, neither heard nor saw anything, nor ever slept more soundly.'

The house was restored completely by Colonel Wildman, and it is now in the hands of Nottingham City Council. The council seems to have escaped the wrath of the Goblin-Monk, although the phantom is still seen with some regularity. Perhaps a council is beyond the reach of even the supernatural. The monk prowls the grounds with his cowl partially pulled up to hide his hideously distorted face, startling visitors and staff from time to time.

In 1966 a cache of medieval treasure was found in what had once been a fishpond just over a mile from the Abbey. Over 1,200 gold coins were unearthed, making this one of the most valuable hoards ever dug up in England. Was this the fabled lost treasure? Probably not, as the coins dated to over a century before the closure of the monastery. In any case the Goblin-Monk remained quiet and failed to haunt – and surely he would know Newstead Abbey treasure.

SHERWOOD FOREST

Sherwood Forest is not what it once was. In the days when Robin Hood and his Merry Men roamed between the trees in search of the rich and corrupt to rob, the forest covered over a hundred square miles. Of this, about 100,000 acres were set aside as a royal forest.

These days, only scattered patches of woodland remain. When the royal forest was sold off, most of the woodland was cleared for farmland. There are several ghosts to be encountered through what was once the mighty Sherwood Forest, but only one is specifically linked to the forest itself.

This strange figure lurks in the denser stands of timber, where he is seen mostly at night. He is said to stand seven feet tall or so and to be dressed entirely in green. His hair and beard are long and untidy, while his eyes are unnaturally large and, at least one witness says, glow with an inner fire. This peculiar apparition is said to wander the paths and byways of the woodland as if searching for something, or someone. For some reason stories about him seem particularly common among courting teenagers who park their cars in the unlit car parks of the forest after dark.

He seems to be some faint echo of the Green Man, formerly a prodigiously powerful nature fairy or pagan deity who stalked the forests of England. In days

A bridleway through Sherwood Forest where a strange and grotesque phantom has been seen.

gone by, when woodlands covered so much of the country, the Green Man was a powerful figure that it was best to avoid. Perhaps with so little native forest left to give him strength, the Green Man is reduced to the alarming, but harmless, figure seen today.

CALVERTON

Calverton is a pretty village, with the main street strung out downhill from west to east. It was once a small hamlet of foresters and gamekeepers who worked in the spreading Sherwood Forest that surrounded the place. Then, in around 1570, the community was transformed when the vicar, William Lee, became annoyed that the young lady whom he was courting would not pay him enough attention. It seemed that the girl in question liked him well enough, for she later married him, but she would keep

The Admiral Rodney pub in Calverton is one of Nottinghamshire's most haunted properties.

knitting stockings for the family business instead of talking to the eager Reverend Lee. Infuriated, Lee set to work inventing a machine for knitting stockings so that his beloved could put down her needles and pay him some attention. The invention proved to be hugely successful. Not only did the future Mrs Lee boost her output, but so did all the other stocking knitters of Calverton. Several of the houses they built as workshops still stand and can be recognised by the wide, shallow, south-facing windows that were built to let in enough light to work by.

By far the most actively haunted site in the village is the Admiral Rodney pub, which stands about halfway along Main Street. At the time the pub was built, the hero of the hour was Admiral George Rodney, who defeated the French in a series of naval actions in the West Indies between 1762 and 1782. So far as is known he never came here, and it is certainly not his ghost that haunts this place.

The first of the spectres goes by the name of Sarah. She is seen only rarely, but her presence is felt more often. She stays down in the large cellar, never venturing up the narrow stairs to the ground floor. Sarah is rumoured to be linked to the underground tunnel that once ran from the cellar to the vicarage. When the vicarage was pulled own, the tunnel was blocked off and now only a patch of differently coloured brickwork shows where it once opened into the pub cellar by way of a heavy wooden door. Was she, perhaps, an illicit girlfriend of a vicar? There are many stories.

What is certain is that she has a sense of humour, and loves modern gadgetry. She will fool around with the electric pumps, taps and chilling equipment that keep the drinks flowing to the bar upstairs. Several times a beer will suddenly stop running, causing the bar staff to run down into the cellar to turn back on a tap or switch that has been turned off by Sarah's phantom hands.

Mr Burns, the landlord in 2004, reported that on one occasion he walked into the cellar just as Sarah was turning off the tap to a large barrel. 'You can write this down,' he said, 'it happened just as certain as you stand there. I walked in and saw the large red tap turning all by itself. Then it stopped. She must have seen me come in.'

The rear corridor of the Admiral Rodney, where the man in black is seen.

Almost as active is the man in black who walks through the rear of the pub. He throws open the back door and slams it shut behind him before walking down a corridor and into the dining area. He is seen often and appears to be dressed in a black suit of 1940s or 1950s styling. This ghost has the knack of being able to open and slam the back door even when it has been firmly locked only a short time earlier.

Although the identity of the man in black is unclear, the elderly gent who is sometimes seen sitting in a corner near the front door sipping a pint of beer is well known. He was a regular at the pub for most of his life until he died just a few years ago. Because his family still lives in the village, it is tactful not to name him, but he is seen clearly and has been recognised by those who knew him in life.

There is no need to wonder why he keeps returning to the Admiral Rodney, for it serves hearty, tasty meals and keeps its beers in excellent condition.

The oldest ghost of Calverton is linked to the old vicarage, though the building no longer stands. At some point in the past, nobody in Calverton is

The modern housing that stands on the site of Calverton's much haunted old vicarage.

entirely certain when, a housemaid in the vicarage hanged herself after being jilted by the coachman just days before her wedding. The coachman then ran off with a girl from Mansfield. It was the sad housemaid's ghost that haunted the house, being seen most often in the front garden close to the gate that opened onto Main Street.

In 1961 the vicarage and its large garden and orchard were sold. The building was scheduled for demolition so that it could be replaced with a Miners' Welfare Club. Only a few days after arriving, the workmen began to report intruders in the property. They said that they heard footsteps shuffling about the place, though they could never find anybody there. At first the noises were put down to mischievous local boys, but after a particularly disturbing encounter in the second week of work this theory was discounted. The foreman refused to give details, but told the management that henceforth his men would work during daylight hours only and that no one would guard the site overnight.

The Miners' Welfare Club too has now gone. The site is today covered by a small housing estate of neat, comfortable family homes. The entrance to the

George Lane in Calverton is home to a terrifying phantom.

cul-de-sac has been the site of several unexplained minor accidents. It seems that motorists pulling into the close suddenly see a figure appear from nowhere in the roadway. They slam on their brakes or swerve to avoid the woman, who strangely cannot then be seen. Perhaps the ghost is still active although her old home, and its replacement, are long gone.

Just up the hill from Old Hall Close, George Lane opens off Main Street, heading south towards Nottingham. It is a long, windy lane that climbs up to the wooded George Hill. Something very strange lurks here. It is variously described as being an old woman in a black dress, a man in a cloak or merely a black shape, and it is sometimes said to wear a silver chain or heavy necklace hanging down on its chest.

This figure is prone to following people down the lane. It will walk close behind them, moving with a strange gliding motion. No matter how quickly the person may walk, or run, the black figure keeps up with them. More than once it has materialised on the back seat of a car, giving the driver a nasty shock and causing at least one to veer off the road. Wherever she or he appears, this indistinct shape exudes a feeling of evil that is quite disturbing.

Further up Main Street there is a stretch of pavement where a ginger-haired man in a tweed jacket is occasionally seen. This is the phantom of a former teacher at the village school who died in one of these cottages before the Great War. He seems happy enough pottering about which is understandable, for Calverton is an attractive village.

GONALSTON

The Old Mill at Gonalston is long gone, and few can have mourned its passing. During the mid-19th century this building was the setting for one of the great social injustices of the era. One that still casts its spectral shadow over the village.

The mill was a large structure that required a large work force. The owner was less than scrupulous, so instead of hiring local men he toured the workhouses of Nottingham and Lincolnshire searching for orphan boys. More particularly, he was looking for workhouse governors whom he could bribe. The workhouse system was not always as bad as it has been painted. It provided basic food and shelter for the truly destitute, and trained children in trades that might help them get jobs as they grew older. One way to do this was for a child to be apprenticed to a local craftsmen. In return for food and bed, though usually nothing more, the child would learn a trade. The workhouse manager would check up on the child every now and then to ensure he was being treated properly.

The millowner of Gonalston took advantage of the system. He would bribe any dishonest manager he found to supply him with orphans whom nobody would miss. These were written off in the workhouse records as having died or been passed to fictional masters. Only a few were ever recorded as going to Gonalston, so the millowner had a far larger work force than he was officially allowed.

For some years the cruel millowner made large sums from working his charges as slave labour and keeping them in miserable conditions. Child mortality was high in those days, but at Gonalston it was horrendous. Those children who

The church at Gonalston was the scene for numerous surreptitious burials.

were officially on his books were buried at Gonalston church in paupers' graves. Those who did not officially exist were dumped in shallow graves on the millowner's property.

Eventually, the villagers grew suspicious of the large numbers of children arriving at the mill and complained to the authorities. The scandal was exposed and the millowner was packed off to a well deserved spell in prison. The mill was demolished, but the graves of the unfortunates were never discovered for nobody knew where they had been buried, nor how many had died. To this day the cries and pitiful moans of the children can be heard in the fields around the church. Perhaps they are crying out for the decent Christian burial that they never received.

THURGARTON

Thurgarton is a Viking settlement in origin – its name means 'farm of Thorgeirr' – and is linked to the pagan god Thor. Despite this, the place was chosen in 1187 as the site for a Benedictine priory dedicated to St Peter. The priory was never one of the larger nor more prosperous in the county, but it did well enough and provided sufficient income to keep its complement of monks supplied while undertaking their spiritual duties. As with so many other religious houses, Thurgarton was closed down by King Henry VIII, its lands and treasures being purloined for royal use.

The old monastic buildings were not torn down, but instead put to use by the local villagers. The priory church was kept as the parish church, while the other buildings became farms, barns and suchlike. Over the years most of the buildings have been rebuilt or demolished and today only the church remains much as it was in medieval times.

The church at Thurgarton is all that remains of the once wealthy priory.

But the church is not the only reminder of the Benedictine monastery, for a ghostly monk in black walks sedately in the grounds. This particular ghost is not seen for very long when he comes visiting. He will appear pacing slowly toward the church with head bowed and arms folded, then step behind a tombstone or bush and be lost to sight. Presumably he cannot bear to be parted from the earthly acre that he once knew so well.

The Saracen's Head at Southwell has a royal ghost.

SOUTHWELL

The charming little town of Southwell is dominated by its vast minster. This was founded as a monastery some time before AD 900, though nobody is sure when, and the magnificent Norman church was begun in 1108. It has seen few changes since it was completed, though it now houses ecclesiastical works from many eras, including perhaps the finest 20th century stained glass window in England. In 1884 the beautifully maintained minster was made a cathedral.

Despite the strong connections to the monastery and original church, there are no phantom monks or friars to be found here. The ghosts are very different creatures, and they congregate at the Saracen's Head hotel facing the minster.

The hotel was founded as the King's Arms in the 12th century. In this guise it played host to King Richard the Lionheart, King John, Henry II and Edward I, among others. When the nearby minster was being dissolved as a monastery, the inn was rebuilt and enlarged using materials salvaged from its earlier self and from the closing monastery. Royalty continued to visit, with James I staying here at least once. The inn entered history more dramatically in August 1642 when King Charles I stayed here on his way to Nottingham where he raised the Royal Standard, signalling the start of the Civil War.

The ancient fireplace in the luxurious King Charles Suite is where the ghostly king is seen most often.

Charles returned to the inn four years later on 4 May 1646, but in very different circumstances. He had now lost the Civil War and was on the run from his own Parliament. Roundhead troopers were hot on his heels, and he stopped at the inn for a single night to rest. It proved to be his last night of freedom before he was captured, imprisoned and eventually executed. He stayed in what is now the King Charles Suite, a cosy room complete with open fireplace, four-poster bed and ensuite facilities.

In 1651 the inn was taken over by a new owner who did not share the Royalist sympathies of the former management. The name of King's Arms was dropped and replaced by the present name. This was a deliberate insult to the Royalists for the king had been beheaded by a Saracen sword. It was soon after this that the ghost of King Charles began to walk, as walk he still does.

He is seen most often in the King Charles Suite, but is sometimes encountered pacing along the narrow corridor that leads to the rooms. As might be expected, considering the grim events that surrounded his visit, the king walks with stooped shoulders and seems dispirited and careworn. The grand clothes and flamboyant fashions that dominate portraits of him are gone. He wears travel-stained garments of coarse wool and boots splashed with mud.

Also haunting this oldest part of the inn is a lady dressed in the fashions of the 18th century. She is a happy ghost, who laughs and smiles as if enjoying some highly amusing jest. In the changes that have been made to modernise the layout of the hotel over the years, the small bedroom where this ghost once appeared has now become the ladies' toilet. The ghost has shocked more than one guest going about her business. Indignation at being interrupted has rapidly given way to surprise at encountering a ghost. But the phantom's good humour seems infectious and nobody appears to mind her intrusion into the modern world.

But the most active of the ghosts at the Saracen's Head is an elderly Regency gentleman. He wears a lovely velvet suit and a powdered wig as he shuffles around the corridors, upstairs and down, giving the impression of looking for something as he moves about. Given his florid complexion, he may be after a late night glass of port.

The receptionist who was on duty as Christmas approached in 2004 had recently done a spell as night porter at the hotel. 'It's a good place this,' he remarked, 'but I tell you straight, when I was on duty as night porter I stayed put at reception unless somebody rang for me. These ghosts are a friendly bunch, but I'm not taking any chances.'

The restaurant had hanging on its wall for a great many years a willow pattern plate that was displayed upside down. Quite how long the plate hung undisturbed is unclear, but it was certainly in place around the time of the Great War. It was known locally as the Plate of Evil, and it was rumoured that bad luck would come to anyone who removed it.

In 2001 the hotel was bought by new owners from outside Southwell who cared little for superstitions surrounding plates. They gave orders that the plate was to be removed as part of the extensive refurbishment that they were

The 'missing window' of the Saracen's Head should be between the two hanging baskets on the first floor.

undertaking. When none of the local workmen would touch the thing, one of the owners removed the plate himself and threw it away. Within weeks the owners ran into serious financial difficulties and had to sell up.

The renovation, however, went on and the hotel was completely updated to provide every luxury a modern traveller could want, but without harming the historic ambience of the place at all. One mystery the refurbishment could not solve, however, is that of the missing window. In the façade of the hotel overlooking the courtyard there is a blank wall where there should, by rights, be a window. Inside the hotel at this point there is a wall of unusual thickness. It has long been rumoured that the wall contains a hidden chamber or priest's hole that may hold some dark secret. After the experience with the Plate of Evil, it was decided to leave well alone and no attempt was made to break the wall down. The mystery remains.

EAST STOKE

Standing astride the Fosse Way, now the A46, a few miles south-west of Newark is the little village of East Stoke. It is, in many ways, typical of Nottinghamshire villages and some might think it unremarkable. But it has its own special place in history. In this village was fought the last battle of the Wars of the Roses.

In 1485 the Battle of Bosworth Field had seen the death of King Richard III of the House of York, and Henry Tudor, the heir to the Lancastrian claims, become King as Henry VII. The Tudor victory was not as decisive as it seems in hindsight. In particular the nephew of Richard, son of the Duke of Clarence, was missing. Although presumed dead he would have been the true heir if found alive.

In 1487 a boy turned up in Ireland claiming to be the missing heir, Edward. The Duchess of Burgundy, his aunt, met him and declared him to be her nephew. Many Irish nobles supported the young man and won to their side several English nobles who had been demoted by Henry VII or were otherwise disgruntled. He was crowned in Dublin as King Edward VI and gathered an army with which to invade England and gain his throne.

The invading army was made up of 2,000 German mercenaries hired by the Duchess of Burgundy, together with 5,000 Irish troops and various English nobles. Chief among these was the Earl of Lincoln. He urged his youthful leader to march to Lincolnshire so that he could rouse the men of his estates to the cause. The invaders got as far as East Stoke before they were caught by King Henry with a royal army some 12,000 strong.

The rebels occupied a hill south-west of East Stoke, looking down on the Fosse Way up which the royal army was approaching. The advance guard of the royal army, led by the Earl of Oxford, had got itself detached from the main body of King Henry's forces. Sensing a chance to destroy the enemy piecemeal, Lincoln ordered an attack. Oxford's men were cut off and surrounded within minutes. The Germans were making steady progress into their front, while the unarmoured Irish swept around their flanks and rear. Fortunately for Oxford, Lord Scales, who was in command of the cavalry of the main body, saw what

*The sombre battlefield of East Stoke where a lone phantom recalls
the last battle of the Wars of the Roses.*

was happening. Without waiting for royal orders or permission, he led his horsemen forward to take the disordered Irish in the rear. For some time savage fighting swayed back and forth over the fields. Then the Irish broke and fled. The Germans realised that defeat was close, but fell back in good order on the church of East Stoke. There they stood, asking for quarter.

King Henry, as was usual for this cautious monarch, reached the battlefield once the fighting was over and sent his cavalry off to slaughter the fleeing Irish. He did not fancy the potentially tough battle against the well-trained German mercenaries, however, so took their surrender on condition that their rebel king was handed over.

When 'King Edward VI' was delivered into the hands of Henry, the truth was quickly discovered. He was not, in fact, the missing prince but the son of a West Country baker. Nevertheless, the boy did look very much like the York family.

Some thought he might be the illegitimate son of one of the notoriously womanising Yorkist leaders and called for his instant execution. Henry, however, had a better idea. He gave the lad a job in the royal kitchens. This said louder than any words that the boy was not of royal stock. If he had been, he would have been executed or imprisoned. By instead giving him a job and freedom, Henry made sure everybody knew that 'Edward VI' was, in fact, the baker's son Lambert Simnel.

Thus ended the Wars of the Roses, but not the echoes of war at East Stoke. A man carrying a long spear or pike is sometimes seen wandering over the old battlefield. He wears what might be a helmet, but otherwise is dressed in a loose jacket and trousers or hose. No doubt this is the ghost of one of the soldiers killed in the fighting and buried outside the church. But on which side he fought and how he met his death, we cannot know.

The beautiful angel of East Stoke.

The churchyard itself has a supernatural mystery of sorts. The most impressive memorial is an imposing angel mounted on a large block of stone. This is the tomb of Baron Julian Pauncefoot, a local landowner of some wealth and the first ambassador that Britain sent to the young United States of America. This angel has been seen to weep on even the driest days. Where the water of the tears comes from – and why – is an enigma.

SOUTH MUSKHAM

I f you are a keen cyclist, it would be as well to be careful when visiting South Muskham. Crow Lane runs from this village to Bathley, twisting and turning as it crosses the farmland. This lane has for many years been the haunt of a phantom hound of truly enormous proportions. With a coat of long, shaggy hair of pure black, this hound runs silently along the lane from South Muskham towards Bathley on some mysterious mission of its own.

For some reason, it has taken a liking to bicycles. During the 20th century the ghostly dog was reported far more often by cyclists than by motorists or walkers.

No real story attaches itself to this hound, but it is remarkably similar to the other spectral black dogs that are to be found all across England. Often known as Shuck, though local names do occur, these animals are generally held to be relics of England's pagan past. Before Christianity came to these shores, the English worshipped a collection of deities that included farmer gods, warrior gods, fertility goddesses and a host of others. Greatest of all was Woden, after whom Wednesday takes its name. This mighty sky god rode into battle on an eight-legged horse, wielding sword and spear and accompanied by a pack of monstrously powerful black dogs.

Crow Lane in South Muskham harbours a most disturbing phantom.

Some people believe that the phantom hounds of England, such as the one patrolling Crow Lane, are hang-over spirits from these ancient gods that have somehow survived into our Christian present.

BESTHORPE

S and Lane at Besthorpe appears to be a quiet, inoffensive sort of a byway. It leaves the village, heading east, takes a sharp left turn, then a right before wandering off across the fields towards Spalford and Wigsley.

There is, however, a quite disturbing secret to be puzzled over here. In the 1840s a windmill stood on the second corner, where it could take advantage of the brisk winds whipping in from the distant coast. The miller was a man named

Sand Lane at Besthorpe, where the ghostly miller is still seen today.

Charlie, who did very well in his business but preferred to live alone and keep others at a distance.

One morning poor Charlie the Miller was found dead in his kitchen, having cut his throat with a carving knife. Nobody had any idea what his troubles were, nor did any emerge after his death. Some sad secret, no doubt, had been gnawing at the man's soul.

But Charlie could not find peace even in death. His ghost soon returned to the mill, walking restlessly around the building and its grounds. Some thought he was looking for something, others that he regretted his actions and sought forgiveness. The mill proved difficult to let and in time was pulled down. But even then Charlie the Miller continued to walk. He is seen today lurking by the side of the road near this corner, staring vacantly towards the site of his old home.

HOLME

The year 1666 was not a good time to live in the village of Holme. Not that there was anything wrong with the place. It was, and is, a perfectly charming hamlet overlooking the River Trent at the end of a lane that leads nowhere except here and peters out in the water meadows alongside the river.

The problem was that death came to Holme that summer in the malevolent form of the plague. This was a dreadful disease that spread terror wherever it went. We know today that it was spread by fleabites from infected rats, but the folk of Holme had no such explanation. All they knew was that the illness apparently came from nowhere to ravage their families.

The disease was horrible. The first sign of infection would be slight swellings in the armpits and groin as the lymph nodes swelled and became infected. The tongue would also swell and become covered in a whitish fur, and fever took rapid hold. Within 24 hours the lymph nodes would swell rapidly to the size of golfballs while the sufferers vomited, ached and began to slur their speech. The following day the fever increased and a stinking brown slime began to ooze from

The parish church of Holme, where a visitation of the plague led to a tragic haunting.

the mouth, while the eyes turned bloodshot and the heartbeat became irregular. On the fourth day the plague fever raged out of control and the lymph nodes turned black with putrid puss and became agonisingly painful. Death usually followed swiftly, only about a quarter of sufferers recovering after a week of such suffering.

Even more dangerous was the pneumonic form of the plague, which infected the lungs. A coughing fit might be followed by specks of blood in the phlegm. Death came in over 95% of cases in less than a day. It was this dreadful disease that struck Holme in the late spring. In a typical attack between a tenth and a third of the population could be expected to fall sick, and most of them would die. Holme was hit far worse than that.

As funeral followed funeral and death stalked the streets, a woman named Nan Scott decided to make her escape from the plague. Believing that the dreadful visitation was a blow from God aimed at her sinful neighbours, Nan decided to cut herself off from her wicked fellow villagers and seek sanctuary in the house of God. She packed up a few clothes and some food, crept into the church and up a narrow flight of stairs to a tiny chamber set in the roof.

There Nan Scott sat as the plague stalked through Holme. She watched as her friends and neighbours died and were buried. Then the village fell silent and still. Running short of food, Nan crept out to search for supplies. Not a living soul remained in Holme. Terrified, she fled back to her refuge, barricaded herself in and waited for death to claim her. And death did come, but not from the plague. She starved to death gradually, too terrified to come out to find something to eat.

It was there that the folk of Holme found her emaciated body some weeks later when they came home. They had not all died, but had fled the infected village to seek their own refuge elsewhere. Given the level of medical knowledge, the people were not to know that the plague had blown itself out. All the infected rats had died and with no humans to feast on, the fleas had died too. Holme was plague free, slowly recovering from the deaths to return to life as the prosperous farming village it had always been.

But Nan Scott's ghost was to return as well. She was glimpsed moving around the churchyard and, most disturbing of all, her footsteps were heard coming from the little chamber while the villagers were in church. The room was blocked up and forgotten, but rediscovered in the later 19th century when a small chest of female clothing was found, along with a plate and mug.

Even today the ghost can be heard walking about in the little room by people in the church, and the pale, frightened figure of Nan Scott is sometimes seen scurrying around the village.

WINTHORPE

For as long as anyone could remember, Winthorpe had been a quiet rural haven just outside the bustling market town of Newark. Then, in 1940, war came to the area in the shape of the hurriedly constructed bomber base of RAF Winthorpe, close beside the Lincoln road.

At first the airfield was just that: a field. The ground was levelled and a few hangars put up, but the landing strip was only grass and the airmen slept in tents, replaced by wooden huts as the winter weather closed in. In those early days the airfield was home to Polish squadrons. These brave men had escaped the Nazi blitzkrieg of 1939 and found their way to Britain. There the RAF equipped them with Wellington bombers and sent them back to war. One of these men was later to return as a ghost, but in Newark cemetery, not here at Winthorpe.

As time passed the airfield was rebuilt with proper concrete runways and stouter, if hardly luxurious, accommodation. Other squadrons moved in, flying the mighty four-engined Stirling and Lancaster bombers that carried heavy bomb loads to pound the German Reich night after night. Inevitably there were many aircraft that failed to return from their missions, and plenty of aircrew who came home only to die of their wounds.

The lane leading into Winthorpe from the north is haunted by a ghost in uniform.

On a dark night in 1944 one Lancaster was limping back to Winthorpe after being damaged by a German nightfighter over the Ruhr. Although badly shot up and limping on three engines, the bomber reached the friendly skies of east Nottinghamshire and lined up for its landing, coming in low from the north-east. What went wrong, nobody knows. The aircraft suddenly veered to the right and plunged into the water meadows of the Fleet Stream. There were no survivors.

It is probably one of the crew of this ill-fated Lancaster that haunts Langford Lane, close to the crash site. He appears quite at ease, walking towards the now abandoned airfield as if returning after an evening out. He is dressed in his air force blue uniform, rather than in flying kit. Perhaps he returns in spectral form to finish off the journey that he was unable to complete in life.

NEWARK

The ancient town of Newark has had more history crammed into its narrow streets than many cities many times the size. Hardly surprisingly, the dramatic events have left their spectral mark.

The site was inhabited in prehistoric times, but it was the Roman era that established Newark as an important town. The Romans built their mighty road, the Fosse Way, to link the powerful fortresses of Lincoln and Exeter, using it as a military highway to move troops rapidly around the island and subdue the native Celtic tribes. At Newark, the Fosse Way ran close to the River Trent at one of the few places where the river could be crossed with any ease. The two routes became economic arteries of later Roman Britain, and the town of Newark prospered accordingly.

After the English conquest Newark declined somewhat, but by the time Lady Godiva, more famous for her naked ride through Coventry, inherited the place it was booming once again. In 1055 Lady Godiva gave the town to the Church. After the Norman conquest the Bishops of Lincoln fortified the hill overlooking the Trent with a wooden castle and in 1125 the present castle was begun. This gave the town its modern name, derived from 'New work', as opposed to the wooden fortification of the old site.

It is a churchman of this period who is the oldest phantom in Newark. Part of the town was given over to the Observant Friars, an order of men noted for being rather more devoted to helping the poor and sick than were many of the more worldly clerics of that age. The friary stood off Appleton Gate, near the northern end of town.

The end for Newark Friary came in 1531. King Henry VIII was in the midst of his dispute with the Pope, but had not yet declared the English Church to be free of Rome with himself as its new head. As part of his dispute, Henry chose to invoke an ancient and obscure law, interpreting it in his own fashion to prove that all the clergymen in England were guilty of colluding with a foreign prince, the Pope. He offered to pardon each of them on payment of cash sums, which were fairly small for each cleric but totalled an impressive £118,840 at the national level.

The friars of Newark gained respect by ministering to the spiritual needs of the poorest in the land.

The friars of Newark discussed the situation and decided that Henry's interpretation of the law was invalid. They refused to pay. The furious King sent a squad of armed men to Newark who arrested Father John Forest and dragged him off to London. Henry wanted to make an example of somebody and that unfortunate proved to be Father Forest. He was executed after the most peremptory of trials.

Two years later, Henry had broken from Rome and was excommunicated. Two more Newark friars chose this inopportune moment to speak out, and were promptly thrown into prison. The friary was seized by the King, closed down and its assets sold for cash to swell the royal coffers.

Exactly which of the friars it is that returns to the site is unclear. By rights, it should be Father Forest, but there is no real proof. The ghost is seen walking slowly, with head bowed, across the grounds of the old friary. He seems to ignore trees and modern structures as if they do not exist. For him, presumably, they don't for he is still following the paths and corridors of the medieval buildings.

In the Civil War of the 17th century, Newark assumed a strategic importance greater than ever before. Cannon were vital to the new style of warfare, and Newark had one of the very few bridges over the Trent that could carry them. The town declared for the King and in February 1643 a Parliamentarian army came to lay

Dashing Prince Rupert led his cavalry to relieve Newark.

siege. The army was driven off with ease by the men of the town, but a second siege began in the autumn and proved to be altogether more serious. It ended on 21st March when the brilliant, if mercurial, Royalist commander, Prince Rupert of the Rhine, marched a relieving army to the rescue.

Prince Rupert rode into the town dressed in his glamorous best and lodged in Kirkgate. He stayed only long enough to accept the profound thanks of the townsfolk and give sound advice on rebuilding the defences before marching off again to continue the war. It would seem, however, that he was around long enough to leave his ghost. A tall, good looking man in Cavalier dress has been seen in the house, now a shop, where he lodged and in the street outside. Whether this is really Prince Rupert, or some other Cavalier, is unclear. Nobody

Kirkgate in Newark, where an old house is haunted by a Cavalier.

has yet managed to get a good enough look at his face to recognise him for certain.

Usually said to date from this same period are the phantom horsemen of Appleton Gate. These ghosts are never seen, but only heard. There appear to be many men getting mounted up amid much clattering of hooves, clashing of steel and jingling of harness. They are said to be Prince Rupert's soldiers mounting up to ride out against the Roundheads. Since nobody has ever seen them, it is impossible to be certain.

The final siege of Newark began on 6 March 1646. At this time Newark was the last town of any real size holding out for the king. It was under siege, not by Oliver Cromwell and the army of Parliament, but by the Scottish army. At that time Scotland was a separate kingdom from England, though it had the same king, and its government was entirely distinct. Scotland was allied to the English Parliament against the English king, and had sent its army to invade England.

The fact that the army besieging the town was foreign added bitterness to the siege and determination to the townsfolk of Newark. The fighting dragged on for weeks, and then for months. The Scots battered the town with cannon, while the garrison fired back, and sallied out to attack the Scots camp. The Scots had to spend time fortifying their camp – they called it 'Edinburgh' – then returned to the attack.

This time they unleashed a secret new weapon. They hired a large force of Scots miners and set them to work to tunnel into the hill on which Newark stood. Working steadily with pick and shovel these men dug secret tunnels under the town, aiming to come up inside the defences. The plan was for Scots soldiers to then pour out of the tunnels, taking the Royalists by surprise, and capture the town.

It was not to be. A small boy heard the strange digging noises, took them for rats and told his father. The father recognised the sounds for what they were. The garrison dug down to meet the Scots, then threw burning straw into the

Newark Market Place, scene of desperate fighting in the Civil War and of modern hauntings.

Barman Stuart stands in the doorway where he was roughly pushed aside by the resident ghost of the Old Kings Arms.

tunnels, followed by boiling water. Few of the miners escaped alive. Then the garrison blocked the tunnels and the bones of the miners were left where they fell.

It is these miners whose ghosts can sometimes be heard in central Newark, particularly in and around the market place. Late at night, when all is quiet and still, the sounds of digging and hacking can be heard clearly coming up from underground.

Newark held out undefeated until, on 8th May, news was brought that the king had been captured. Realising that further bloodshed was pointless, the town agreed to surrender to Parliament on condition that the Scots were not allowed into the town. The Civil War was over.

War was to come to Newark again three centuries later when the Second World War brought German bombers overhead to pound the town and its industry. On 7th March 1941 a heavy raid battered the area around the railway station, demolishing several buildings. One woman was never found; perhaps she had been blown to pieces or buried so deep that nobody dug down far enough. Ever since that fatal night the poor lady's ghost has been seen wandering around the area. It is thought she may be trying to lead the living to her body so that she can be properly buried, but to date nobody has followed her to find out.

Other ghosts in Newark are more difficult to date. Typical is the grumpy old man who haunts the Old Kings Arms in Kirkgate. The pub gained its name in 1820 when popular King George III died and his son ascended the throne as George IV. The landlord of the time so disliked the wastrel George IV, that he dubbed his pub the Old Kings Arms to associate it with the previous monarch.

The pub's ground floor is much as it has been for centuries, but what used to be the first floor living quarters for the landlord have now been converted to be a restaurant and kitchens. It is here that the pub serves its hearty meals, as opposed to the snacks served in the bar. And it is here that the grumpy old man makes himself a nuisance. He will stomp about bad temperedly, moving furniture, switching off lights and slamming doors. One afternoon in 2001 the barman was tidying up after lunch when he heard the ghost approach him from behind and then push him roughly aside.

The Woolpack pub, which may be haunted by a grey lady.

The cellar is also said to be haunted, but this ghost has never been seen and the phenomenon seems to be little more than something that gives intruders a spooky feeling of being watched.

Similarly difficult to pin down is the grey lady said to haunt the Woolpack pub. She is seen sometimes in the main bar, walking through as if she owns the place. Perhaps she once did, but her identity remains unknown.

Although the precise name of the ghost at Newark cemetery is obscure, it is easy to know something about him. This large cemetery on the A46 outside town is approached through impressive gates. As well as holding a good number of the worthy townfolk, the cemetery is the last resting place for many of the airmen who served on bases around the area during the Second World War, but were killed or died of natural causes.

It is one of these airmen who haunts the cemetery, walking slowly among the tombstones and wearing an RAF uniform of blue. It is thought that he may be Polish, for he is seen most often in the Polish section of the graveyard. If so, he may have served at RAF Winthorpe as that base held Polish squadrons for much of the war. He is a ghost who is a long way from home.

BALDERTON

B alderton was once a separate village, but is now a suburb of Newark. It was linked to the town as the populations of both boomed in Victorian times and now seems to be almost one with its larger neighbour, though residents are clear that Balderton retains a distinct village atmosphere.

It no longer has its hospital, closed down in 1993 as part of economy measures and now used as offices. Many of the buildings are earmarked for demolition so that the site can be redeveloped for housing. Fortunately for the ghosts, the older heart of the hospital, the fine mansion of Balderton Hall, is not to be demolished. The house was built in 1840 by a prosperous local banker, Thomas Godfrey, and stayed in the family until 1880, after which it became home to some of Newark's more wealthy citizens.

The more active of the ghosts date from the Godfrey years. The first is a little girl who plays in the corridor at the top of the stairs. She has long blonde hair and gambols about quite happily before fading from view. Rather less content are the two elderly ladies who haunt the main hall. Not that they are at all unhappy, they just seem to be rather sombre as they stroll through the building in their long, high-necked dresses of thick bluish wool.

Appearing rather less often is the phantom seen in the grounds. This is a tall, strapping young man dressed in the wartime uniform of the United States Army Air Force. He strides purposefully across the lawns and paths as if on some determined mission from so long ago. Nobody is sure exactly who he is, but the hospital buildings were requisitioned in 1942 to act as accommodation and social buildings for the increasing numbers of American airmen who were being based at the RAF stations around Newark. It must be one of these gallant fliers who returns to Balderton, perhaps to the last home he knew on Earth.

•South Nottinghamshire•

ARNOLD

The broken monument that records the royal past of Bestwood Lodge.

S tanding right on the northern edge of the Nottingham spread of suburbs is the little town of Arnold. And on the edge of Arnold is the mighty mansion and spreading grounds of Bestwood Lodge.

As a broken stone monument in the grounds records, this was a prosperous and profitable manor granted by King Charles II to the first Duke of St Albans.

It was no normal grant of land from a monarch to a favoured subject, however, for the Duke was the illegitimate son of the king by that famous actress Nell Gwynne.

The affair between Charles and Nell began in 1668 when Charles asked Nell out for a meal after attending one of the sparklingly witty comedies in which she specialised. As the meal ended, the innkeeper brought the bill to Nell as she was the only person he recognised around the table. She passed the bill to the king, but he had no money so passed it to his brother, the Duke of York. Not having enough in his purse, York pushed the bill to the final person present, Sir Charles Villiers. 'Oddsfish,' laughed Nellie, 'but this is the poorest company I have ever kept.' The incident was at once written into the play.

Although he had other mistresses, Charles never threw Nell Gwynne aside. Indeed, his dying words in 1685 were to his brother, soon to become King James II. 'Let not poor Nellie starve,' muttered Charles. James didn't.

The site of the old hunting lodge at Arnold, now a hotel, has a very jolly ghost indeed.

In fact, there was little danger of the former actress from Hereford living in poverty. She had had two children by King Charles. The younger boy, James, died in childhood but the elder, Charles Beauclerk, grew to be a strapping and popular adult. Charles gave him the title 'Duke of St Albans' and granted him estates suitable to this new station in life. Bestwood Lodge was one of these.

Together the teenage Duke and his mother oversaw the building of a hunting lodge on the estate where they could retire from London for some quiet days in the country. Nellie, at least, seems to have enjoyed her time at Bestwood, so much, in fact, that she has never left. To this day a lady dressed in the fashions of the later 17th century is often seen walking through the grounds. No quiet ghost this. She laughs and chats to invisible companions as if in the happiest of moods, and is generally taken to be Nell Gwynne enjoying the afterlife as much as she enjoyed her mortal life.

The house built by the first Duke has not survived, the modern grand structure being mostly 19th century in date. It is now a hotel, but spent both world wars as a military hospital. Some years ago a limping soldier dressed in the uniform of the Great War was seen several times in the upper corridors of the house. The present staff know nothing about him, so this ghost presumably proved to be less enduring than the lady in the grounds.

GUNTHORPE

The River Trent at Gunthorpe, north-east of Nottingham, flows wide and deep. The bridge here is the only crossing point between Nottingham and Newark and now carries the A6097. The village lies off the main road, with broad water meadows running down to the river.

It is across these water meadows that a strange, phantom animal has been

The River Trent at Gunthorpe, home to a mysterious phantom creature.

seen to run as dusk closes in. Some witnesses liken it to a gigantic cat or panther bounding across the grassland. Others think it is a large dog lolloping along. Whatever it is, the spectral beast is in sight for only a second or two before it vanishes into thin air.

Like the other ghosts of Nottinghamshire, the phantom cat of Gunthorpe goes about its business without bothering too much with the modern, mortal inhabitants of the county. These spectres have their own reasons for walking Nottinghamshire, and it is not for us to bother them with our presence.

NOTTINGHAM

The city of Nottingham owes its existence to a steep sandstone bluff that dominates the River Trent at this spot. In AD 920 King Edward the Elder built a fortified town on the hill to block the use of the Trent by Vikings rowing upstream to raid and pillage central England.

The gatehouse is the only survivor of the powerful medieval fortress of Nottingham Castle.

When the Normans conquered the country, King William I moved the town down to a lower section of the hill and replaced it with a mighty royal castle. This was built as much to intimidate the local English into submission as it was to dominate the Trent. In 1154 the castle was rebuilt by Henry II, but it was his two sons whose story pushed Nottingham into legend. King Richard the Lionheart went on crusade, whereupon his brother John seized control of Nottingham Castle as part of his bid for power. The vast expanse of Sherwood Forest to the north became a refuge for those fleeing John's harsh taxes and cruel injustices. There, according to later legend, they were led by Robin Hood, Little John, Friar Tuck and other characters.

The castle ghost, however, dates from 1330. In that year in the castle a dramatic coup took place that overthrew an illegal regime and put the rightful king back on the throne. In 1327 the inept and unpopular Edward II had been murdered by his own wife, Queen Isabel, and her lover Roger Mortimer, Earl of March. The couple proclaimed Edward's son to be King as Edward III, but in fact kept power for themselves. They proved to be far more competent than the king they had killed, but also spectacularly corrupt and tyrannical.

In 1330, the young Edward III decided he had to take action against his mother and Mortimer to assert his own rule and restore justice and honesty to government. There was no lack of support for him among the nobility, but Mortimer was cunning and careful. He kept a large body of armed Welsh mercenaries close to him at all times and slept only when locked securely in a castle with his opponents on the outside.

But on 19th October a Grand Council was due to be held in Nottingham Castle. As usual, Mortimer ensured that those nobles he suspected were lodged in the town, while his Welshmen guarded the walls and gates of the castle. Edward, however, had his own plan. He was lodged in the castle where Mortimer could keep an eye on him. With Edward, himself just 17, were various teenage sons of the noble families of England who served as Edward's friends and household officials. Edward knew these boys would be no match for Mortimer's tough mercenaries, but most of them were guarding the gates and walls. Edward hoped to be able to overpower the few who guarded Mortimer himself.

At midnight the group of teenagers crept through the darkened castle, armed with daggers and knives. They arrived without incident outside Mortimer's chamber and Edward demanded instant admittance. The three guards at the door refused, so the boys leapt at them. The fight was soon over, but the alarm had been given. Edward rushed into Mortimer's room to find him alone with the Chancellor discussing tax revenues. He sent a group of boys off to open the gates and admit the waiting nobles and their men, while he barricaded himself into the room and waited rescue or death, whichever came first.

Queen Isabel was awake by this point and threw herself at the door behind which Edward held Mortimer prisoner. 'Fair son, Fair son,' she wailed, 'have pity on gentle Mortimer.' Distraught with worry, the queen turned frantic with fear when the sounds of armed men marching up the corridor reached her ears. She fled into the night, racing round the castle grounds in vain search for escape. She was found at dawn, a gibbering wreck hiding in a wooden outhouse.

Edward had Mortimer promptly put before a jury of his enemies, condemned to death and hanged as a common criminal. His mother was packed off to a

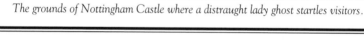

The grounds of Nottingham Castle where a distraught lady ghost startles visitors.

convent where she spent the rest of her life. She never recovered from that night in Nottingham Castle, however, and she talked endlessly of its terrors.

Even in death, Queen Isabel could not escape the horrors of Nottingham Castle. Almost as soon as she died, her ghost was seen in the grounds, gibbering in terror or calling out the name of her lover Mortimer. Although the medieval castle has almost completely vanished, to be replaced with a comfortable Georgian mansion, her ghost still wanders outside. Clad in a nightdress of cream silk she darts hither and thither in obvious fear and grief.

Such are the desserts of murder and treason.

* * *

Close outside the castle stands an ancient building which claims to be the oldest pub in England. This is Ye Olde Trip to Jerusalem. It was built in 1189 to serve as a gathering place for Nottinghamshire men preparing to go on crusade, and also as an inn for paying guests when the crusading spirit flagged.

The ghosts of this pub are strangely insubstantial. Down in the cellar there is a man who is heard more often than seen. He stomps about as if wearing heavy boots, but otherwise does not seem to cause much bother. More disturbing is the model galleon that hangs from the ceiling. As any visitor can see, it is thickly coated in dust. This is because a former landlord is said to have laid a curse upon the thing, which would bring bad luck to anyone who touched it. The reasons for the curse are unknown and, since the staff won't touch it, nobody knows if the curse has any real power.

What is claimed to be the oldest pub in England boasts a ghost and a curse.

A little down the hill from the castle, and across the modern ring road that cuts it off from the city centre, stands Ye Olde Salutation Inn. This pub dates back to 1240, though most of what stands today dates from the 15th century. It is said to hide two ghosts within its welcoming walls.

A ghost appeared in Bridlesmith Gate after building work uncovered an ancient secret.

The older is that of a highwayman who was arrested there in the 1730s. Appearing to recreate the last moments before the forces of justice prevailed,

The Old Angel Inn has been modernised, but no amount of change can get rid of the phantom.

he leaps to his feet brandishing a pair of pistols and shouting silent oaths of defiance at invisible attackers, then he vanishes.

The second ghost is less dramatic. This is the phantom of a former landlord who died on the premises, apparently after accidentally poisoning himself. He is glimpsed going about the normal business of a landlord from time to time.

Further into the city centre is the old street of Bridlesmith Gate. In 1969 one of the shops in this street was undergoing refurbishment. The workmen in the cellar accidentally broke though into what had obviously been a cave or cellar, but which had been blocked up for many decades. It was not even clear to which property the chamber had originally belonged. Soon afterwards a man dressed in a

A modern nightclub was once home to an ancient spirit.

long, dark coat and wearing a wide-brimmed hat began to be seen in the street. Who he was and what his links were to the hidden chamber, nobody can tell. He appears still, so perhaps one day a person braver than the rest may ask him.

Also in the old town centre is the Old Angel Inn. This pub has recently been updated to include the sorts of features that appeal to the youthful tastes of Nottingham's large student population, though the ancient fabric was left largely untouched. Also undisturbed was the unseen phantom who sings gently to herself when the pub is quiet.

The Works Nightclub occupies part of a large modern building that also includes a multiplex cinema, several restaurants and extensive offices. Soon after it was built a poltergeist took up residence. Doors were thrown open, objects went missing and staff often felt as if an invisible presence were watching them. Whoever, or whatever, was responsible must have found the music too loud, for it has now gone and the club is free from supernatural activity.

The Loggerheads pub lies right at the foot of the hill on which the castle and old city are built. Inside this hostelry is said to lurk the ghost of a soldier who seems to date from the First World War period and is probably an officer. He is encountered in the downstairs bar. Upstairs is the preserve of a jolly little Victorian girl who plays along the corridors and darts in and out of rooms.

The old courthouse in Nottingham hides some dark secrets.

The nearby tourist attraction, the Galleries of Justice, occupies the old court rooms and city lockup. The ghost, if that is what it is, lurks in the rooms hollowed out of the sandstone rock beneath the building and seems to be that of a woman who is panting or sobbing, but she is seen infrequently and rarely in any detail.

Running west from the city centre is the A52, Derby Road. This road is haunted by an AA patrolman dating back to the 1930s. Riding his motorbike and dressed in the uniform of the time, he zips by as if on his way to a call.

WILFORD

The village of Wilford has been almost completely engulfed by the spreading suburbs of Nottingham, though it does retain something of its own character and ambience. It also has its own ghosts.

In the 1980s the Ferry Inn hit the national headlines after the pub landlady got so fed up with the antics of the resident ghost that she called in an exorcist. It was never entirely clear who this ghost was, but he was most active. He slammed doors, threw them open again and stomped about the place in a loud and unpleasant manner. Staff saw glasses and other objects move by themselves, a pint glass once gliding silently from one end of the bar to the other in front of a barmaid's astonished eyes. The exorcism would seem to have been successful for the trouble has now ceased.

Still very much around is the ghost at the Wilford power station. This is George, the ghost of a man who worked in the power station from when he left school until he retired. The ghost of the old boy, dressed in his usual overalls and with a flat cap pulled down to shade his eyes, began to be seen soon after his death.

The phantom that was frequently spotted at the ambulance station at Wilford was not so easily identified, for the simple reason that nobody ever managed to get a good look at him. He was dressed in a jacket, perhaps a suit, but was only glimpsed for a second or two at a time. One clear sighting from the 1980s came when an ambulance driver saw the man, whom he took for a visitor, enter the gents' toilet. Wanting to use the amenities himself, the driver waited patiently outside. When the man had not re-emerged ten minutes later, the man knocked, then entered to find the room totally empty.

WOLLATON HALL

Lying on the western edge of Nottingham is the imposing edifice of Wollaton Hall. This mighty mansion was built in the 1580s by Sir Francis Willoughby in the latest fantasy style with pinnacles, arches, towers and turrets. It is now in the care of the city council, which has installed its history museum within the house and opened the extensive grounds to the public as a park.

The most active of several ghosts at Wollaton Hall is that of Lady Middleton, who haunts Room 19. This now houses a collection of fossils, but when the Hall was a private house it was the bedroom of the unfortunate lady herself. In middle age Lady Middleton fell down

Wollaton Hall, now a museum, has a ghost in what was once a bedroom.

the stairs, breaking her back and became paralysed from the waist down. She was taken to her bedroom and rarely left it for the rest of her life.

The ghost of this lady is gentle enough. She stands staring out of a window or walks slowly through the chamber, ignoring any mere mortals who happen to be present. As frequently appearing as the ghost herself, is the phantom candlelight that can be seen twinkling through the ancient windows of the room after dark by those who are in the park.

The grounds of Wollaton Hall were, in the 1970s, the venue for some most peculiar sightings. The apparitions were of little men who were seen moving about the lower parts of the park. Some thought they must be the occupants of flying saucers, though no UFOs were ever seen. Others maintained that the sightings were of the little people, fairies and the like. Most dismissed them as nonsense. Whatever their origins, the little men were witnessed off and on for some months, then they seemed to tire of Wollaton and have not been seen since.

COLWICK HALL

The beautiful Georgian mansion of Colwick Hall lies close to the River Trent, on the southern outskirts of Nottingham. A manor is recorded on this site in the Domesday Book of 1086 when it was owned by William Peverel, the Norman governor of Nottingham Castle.

During the 14th century the manor was bought by the Byron family, which later acquired the much haunted Newstead Abbey. In 1643 the Byrons sold Colwick Hall to Sir John Musters, whose family remained there for many generations. It is perhaps ironic that it was one of these Musters that Lady Mary Ann Chaworth married after her family rejected the suit of the Lord Byron who then found great fame as a poet.

It is this lady whose ghost haunts the house and grounds to this day.

The Hall was subjected to a violent attack during the Reform Bill riot of 1831. John Musters was a known opponent of the bill and his home was targeted by the rioters when the bill was rejected by the House of Lords. On Monday,

10th October, a mob gathered in the Market Square in Nottingham, and the 15th Hussars were called from the Park Barracks to disperse them. One section eluded the soldiers and made its way through Sneinton to Colwick Hall, where the rioters hacked their way

The façade of Colwick Hall, now a welcoming hotel on the outskirts of Nottingham.

into the house with axes, ransacked the wine cellar and many of them became drunk. Nearly every window was broken, many valuable paintings were destroyed including works by Titian, Rubens and Canaletto, china and glass were smashed, furniture broken up and the grand piano demolished. Fires were started in many of the rooms but an attempt to ignite some gunpowder failed because it had been allowed to get wet. Mrs Musters, together with her daughter and a French lady visitor, hid from the mob in a nearby shrubbery; Mr Musters was away from home. It was claimed that Mrs Musters' life was cut short because of this experience. She died four months later.

The house and grounds are now a hotel offering fine foods and hospitality. The current house dates from the early 18th century, but extensive alterations made in 1776 completely changed its appearance. The architect, John Carr of York, built his design around the original square building. The south front was totally rebuilt and extended on both sides by the addition of two one-storey wings. The interior still

The ghost of Colwick Hall glides silently along a corridor.

contains some original fireplaces and cornices designed by Carr in the Adam style. The stables and kennels at the side were added in 1778.

Colwick Hall also offers the ghost of the unfortunate Mrs Chaworth-Musters. She is seen in the grounds, hiding behind trees and lurking in the shadows as she must have done on that awful day in 1831. She also frequents the interior of her old home, particularly the east wing. It was here that the ghost was photographed as it glided along a corridor. The hotel had hired a photographer to take pictures for a brochure, so he was on hand to snap the ghost as it began to fade from view.

WEST BRIDGFORD

Like many villages around Nottingham, West Bridgford is now almost a suburb. It retains its own character and high street, but the network of roads is continuous into the city.

Down towards the river, near the famous Trent Bridge cricket ground, stands the Lady Bay public house. During the 1970s and early 1980s the pub seemed to be bothered by a visitation of strange, ghostly activity. The figure of a man wearing a cloak was glimpsed infrequently in the car park, while inside the building lights would be flicked on and off by invisible hands.

The Lady Bay pub at West Bridgford, where all is now quiet.

Today the ghost does not seem to be very active. Certainly he does nothing to detract from enjoyment of the fine meals and drinks on offer.

ATTENBOROUGH

U ntil fairly recently, Attenborough was a small village isolated by the broad marshes and floodlands around the River Trent south of Nottingham. Today most of the wetlands have been drained and the village is now virtually a suburb of Nottingham. Some extensive marshes remain south and east of the village, however, and it is here that the ghosts are to be found.

They are seen often enough for them to be identified reasonably well. Riding their horses down to the Trent at Barton-in-Fabis, they urge their mounts into the water at what was a ford until the river was dredged in the 19th century. On the other side, they emerge close to Attenborough church, then fade from sight. These are without doubt Parliamentary troopers from the time of the English Civil War. They wear the lobster-pot helmets and breastplates of the era, and have long, heavy swords dangling by their sides.

Attenborough was home to the Ireton family, who were among the stoutest supporters of Parliament in Nottinghamshire. The eldest brother, Henry, was a cavalry commander of great talent. He fought at Edgehill and Naseby, as well as at numerous skirmishes and sieges. In 1646 he married Bridget, daughter of Oliver Cromwell, and some expected him to succeed Cromwell as Lord Protector of the English Republic, but his death in 1651 ensured this did not happen. The younger brother, John, served in the Parliamentarian army without achieving high rank. He was imprisoned when Charles II regained his throne, but was soon released to return home to Attenborough.

It seems likely that the ghosts date from early in the Civil War. The Ireton brothers raised a regiment of local men and based them in Attenborough where the surrounding wetlands

Roundhead troopers haunt the riverbanks at Attenborough.

meant they would not be surprised by a Royalist attack. The horses were stabled in the church, which the Puritan Iretons took to be mere mortal frippery compared to the unknowable splendour of God. From this refuge the Ireton regiment rode out to harass local Royalists, to secure stocks of arms and money for Parliament and generally make nuisances of themselves.

The activity did not last long. With Nottingham firmly for the king, Attenborough soon proved to be a dangerous place. Casualties were high and the Iretons rode off to join the main Parliamentary army further south.

Presumably the ghostly Roundheads crossing the Trent at Attenborough are men who joined the Iretons, but who paid with their lives for their support of Parliament. Perhaps their ghosts follow the route covered by their bodies as their comrades took them back to Attenborough for burial.

RUDDINGTON

The ghost at Ruddington was once extremely active, but has not been seen for a good few years. Some ghosts do this. They appear frequently and regularly for a while and then quickly fade away, never to be seen again. Perhaps they have burned up whatever energy they had in a burst of frenetic activity, while other phantoms appear less often but for longer periods of time.

The bakery in Ruddington where a ghost used to be seen with great frequency.

Reports of this phantom from the 1950s and 1960s are numerous and detailed, though by the 1970s he was being seen less often and seems to have vanished completely sometime in the 1980s. Today he is barely a memory.

He was a tall man dressed in a casual blazer and tie with flannel or cotton trousers. He was said to be middle-aged with hair greying at the sides, and had a confident stride. The spectre would walk up Church Street to reach the Horspools Bakery, which still exists and offers fine bread and tasty snacks to the people of Ruddington. One account says he walked into the bakery, but others do not mention this.

Whatever route he took, the ghost appeared to be quite solid and real – until he suddenly vanished into thin air. An interesting phantom, which is now gone.

BUNNY

The delightfully named Bunny is as charming a village as its name might suggest. But this is no haphazard collection of buildings thrown up over time by the good folk of Nottinghamshire – instead it was one of the very first fully planned villages in England.

As a young man, Baron Sir Thomas Parkyns travelled widely. He had the wealth and the inclination to do so. Unlike many men of his time, however, Sir Thomas scorned the 'Grand Tour' of European capitals and instead travelled the length and breadth of 17th century England. In Cornwall he learned to wrestle, and found he loved the sport. Thereafter wherever the strapping young nobleman stopped he would challenge the local lads to a wrestling match. It was said that he hired as servants only men who had beaten him in a wrestling match.

Eventually, of course, the responsibilities of the family estates beckoned and Sir Thomas returned home to Bunny. He decided that his lands and tenants would be the finest in England. To that end he set about completely rebuilding the village and his home, Bunny Hall. Almshouses and a school were put up, as well as new farms and improved roads. The church was just about the only building that Sir Thomas left alone, perhaps out of reverence for the Almighty. Of course, Sir Thomas challenged all the workmen to wrestling matches and was soon known throughout Nottinghamshire and beyond as the Wrestling Baron and an amiable eccentric.

As he grew older, Sir Thomas took up another hobby unusual among the gentry of the time: stone coffins. He loved them. Whenever one was dug up – as they were from time to time when graves were being dug in ancient churchyards – Sir Thomas would ride over at high speed to inspect it. He would usually offer the parish authorities a good sum of money to buy the curiosity, which was then carted back to Bunny to be stored in the parish church.

In 1741 he passed away and was buried in the old church at Bunny. His monument had already been completed and put in place some years earlier, so that Sir Thomas could contemplate his own mortality when at prayer. It shows him standing in wrestling pose, but beside this fine sculpture is another showing him flat on his back at the foot of Old Father Time. The inscription reads: 'That time at length did throw him is plain.'

Time has not, however, stopped him from walking round Bunny to admire his handiwork and to ensure that his successors at the Hall have kept up his standards. Wearing a long coat festooned with gold braid and ornate buttons, the Wrestling Baron is spotted pootling about various parts of the village. He seems especially fond of the almshouses for some reason.

There are other ghosts at Bunny. A former gardener has been seen several times in the grounds of Bunny Hall, which remains a private house, and a kindly elderly couple have been seen on more than one occasion near the church. Compared to the dominating personality of the Wrestling Baron, however, such phantoms are pale indeed.

FOSSE WAY

The lonely ghost who trudges endlessly along the A46 near Owthorpe has become a familiar figure to motorists – though it is likely many do not realise that the shuffling form is anything other than a local in fancy dress. It is possible, however, that he may help solve one of the enduring mysteries of Roman Britain.

In AD 61 Boadicea, Queen of the Iceni, led her tribe in rebellion against the harsh rule of Rome. The Romans had invaded Britain barely 20 years earlier and established a firm grip only on the south-east of the island. The Iceni of Norfolk were allies of Rome, but after the death of their king, Prasutagus, the Romans decided to annex the territory, strip the nobles of their wealth and impose high taxes on the farmers. When Boadicea objected, she was stripped naked, flogged and her daughters raped. The Romans may have thought the brutality would put the Iceni queen in her place. In fact it only roused her anger.

The Iceni marched to war, soon joined by the Trinovantes of Suffolk and Essex. The largest Roman city in Britain at the time was Colchester, so Boadicea fell on the city, burned it to the ground and slaughtered around 30,000 Romans.

The Roman governor of Britain, Suetonius Paulinus, was campaigning in North Wales at the time. He at once abandoned the campaign and marched his legion south-east along the newly completed Watling Street, now the A5. At the same time he sent messengers to the legionary commanders at the fortresses of Exeter and Lincoln to march along the Fosse Way, now the A46, to meet him where the two roads crossed near modern Warwick.

Quintus Petillius Cerialis duly marched out of Lincoln, heading south-west. He had with him most of his IX Legion, though garrisons had been left behind at Lincoln and other forts. Somewhere along the Fosse Way he was ambushed by Boadicea and her warriors. The legion was cut to pieces and most of the men killed. Cerialis escaped on horseback, and two days later he was back at Lincoln, barricading the gates and hurriedly improving the fortifications. Boadicea chose not to follow him, but instead sacked London before meeting Paulinus in battle and being defeated.

Exactly where disaster engulfed the IX Legion has long been a puzzle. It took Cerialis and his surviving horsemen two days to get back to Lincoln, which might indicate the distance of the battlefield from that city. However, we do not know if the men were riding at full speed up the Fosse Way or instead spent most of their time hiding from the Celtic warriors in dense woodland. Some believe Cerialis got beyond Leicester, others that he had barely left Lincoln.

And so to the ghost. The figure seen stumbling along the roadside is heading north, towards Lincoln. He wears what looks like a helmet and what some take to be a heavy jacket or coat. Only one witness, so far as can be discovered, has said the coat is mail, as opposed to cloth, but all agree on its obvious weight. The man carries neither shield nor weapon.

Is he a Roman fugitive of the IX Legion? His dress certainly sounds like that of a legionary stripped of his shield and weapons, which a man fleeing instant and bloody death would throw aside in his haste to run away. And he is heading towards safety at Lincoln. If so, this ghost would locate the battlefield somewhere on the wolds between Cotgrave and Leicester. It would have been good country for an ambush.

On the other hand this sad phantom might be a fugitive from some other forgotten battle from the Dark Ages. Until somebody gets a good enough look at this strange ghost the truth will have to remain uncertain.

COLSTON BASSETT

Colston Bassett is best known these days for the delicious Stilton cheese that is made there. The dairy, a little north of the village, sells the cheese direct to passers-by, along with the less well known White Stilton and some Shropshire Blue that is just as tasty. The village ghosts, however, have a distinctly religious flavour.

In 1892 the Lady of the Manor, Lady Alice Millington, passed away at a tragically young age. Her distraught husband, Sir Robert, sought a suitable memorial for her and found it when he looked at the tumbledown state of the parish church. St Mary's had been begun in Norman times on a small hill above the River Smite. As Colston Bassett increased in population and prosperity the church had been steadily enlarged until it had two large aisles as well as the usual nave, transepts and choir.

Then came the enclosure acts of the 16th and 17th century, which revolutionised agriculture in England. In some areas, these led to a boom in rural wealth, but in Colston Bassett they caused only economic hardship and a drastic fall in population. Like other villages in the beautiful Vale of Belvoir, Colston Bassett saw its youngsters move to Nottingham, Grantham and even

London in search of jobs. The village church soon became too large for the congregation and too expensive to maintain. And as the village shrank, people preferred to live nearer to the Smite, so the church was left isolated on its hill. The north aisle was pulled down, but even then keeping the remaining fabric in good condition was a constant problem. By the time Lady Alice died, the church was in a terrible condition.

Rather than spend his money on the tumbledown St Mary's, Sir Robert decided to build a completely new church. He bought a plot in the village centre and on it erected St John's in

The ruined church of Colston Bassett has not been abandoned by its former congregation.

the very latest Gothic taste. The church is magnificent, with a 150-ft spire, stone arcades, slender pillars and a wealth of carving. One of these, a life-sized angel in marble, is a portrait of the deceased Lady Alice.

Meanwhile, the old church on the hill was left to decay. To save it from profane use, the Church authorities tore off the roof and left the interior open to the elements. It stands still, a gaunt and roofless ruin that still maintains an air of dignity and sacred peace among the fields.

One of the glassless windows of Colston Bassett church through which phantom lights twinkle late at night.

When the wind blows over the Nottinghamshire countryside, the church bells of St Mary's swing gently in the air, their clappers letting out a doleful chiming. This is odd, as the bells were removed many years ago. And yet many villagers claim to have heard the old church bells ringing up on the hill. Those who pass this way after dark have seen candlelight coming from the ruined church, and one local who stopped his car to get a better look was certain he heard a hymn being sung as if by a fair sized congregation. Suddenly the lights went out and silence fell.

The modern parishioners may choose to worship at St John's in the village centre, but it would seem that the congregations of times past prefer to stay up on the hill in their old church.

• Index •